ISBN 978-0-428-11410-7
PIBN 11247221

1 MONTH OF
FREE
READING

at

www.ForgottenBooks.com

By purchasing this book you are eligible for one month membership to ForgottenBooks.com, giving you unlimited access to our entire collection of over 1,000,000 titles via our web site and mobile apps.

To claim your free month visit:
www.forgottenbooks.com/free1247221

English
Français
Deutsche
Italiano
Español
Português

www.forgottenbooks.com

Mythology Photography **Fiction**
Fishing Christianity **Art** Cooking
Essays Buddhism Freemasonry
Medicine **Biology** Music **Ancient**
Egypt Evolution Carpentry Physics
Dance Geology **Mathematics** Fitness
Shakespeare **Folklore** Yoga Marketing
Confidence Immortality Biographies
Poetry **Psychology** Witchcraft
Electronics Chemistry History **Law**
Accounting **Philosophy** Anthropology
Alchemy Drama Quantum Mechanics
Atheism Sexual Health **Ancient History**
Entrepreneurship Languages Sport
Paleontology Needlework Islam
Metaphysics Investment Archaeology
Parenting Statistics Criminology
Motivational

Foreword

In the years to come, if what you read in this edition of the Yucca fans into flame the smouldering fires of memory and enables you to recall the activities and the pleasant associations of this college year, our efforts will not have been in vain.

The Staff

Dedication

To J. W. Pender

Whose labors among us have demonstrated that he is a Christian gentleman, a one hundred per cent American, an example for all students with whom he has come in contact to catch up the torch of democracy and bear it on — This volume of the Yucca is respectfully dedicated to— "just Dad".

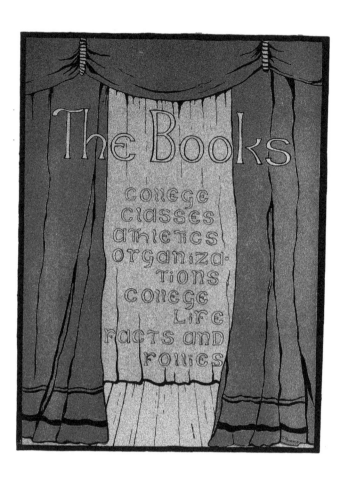

The Books

College
Classes
Athletics
Organiza-
tions
College
Life
Facts and
Follies

To The Eagle

Chaucer, who piped in that rare morning song
    Of English verse, "The Parlement of Foules,"
Sang of thee, and shall I do thee wrong
    To follow where he led? Not so. This school
Where youths and maidens oft in numbers meet
    To watch thy foster children try their skill
In feats of strength or quickness, or to greet
    Their friendly enemies in contests, will
Enshrine thee as her totem. Thy keen eye
    Shall see upon her field of combat none
Who are not meet to join thee in the sky,
    Who have not earned their places in the sun.
Blest Eagle with the upward look, know we
    Aspire to all that's lofty, like to thee.

                                        B. S.

OUR COLLEGE SONG

Words-Charles Langford

Music-Julia Smith

1. We're right behind our college in every thing she does, For we
2. We're with her on the platform; we're with her on the court; We're

know we'll never find her in the wrong; We believe in her standards, and we'll
with her on the field the whole day long; She always stands the test, and we'll

ever give her praise, and for her we'll forever sing this song.
always love her best, and for her we'll forever sing this song.

chorus
Singing

glory to the green, singing glory to the white, For we

know our dear old college is forever in the right; Down the

corridor of years we'll forget the joys and tears, But the Normal, the Normal, we love

The Eagle

NOT ONLY is the Eagle the king of the air, but he has been con-·
sidered by more than one nation as a fitting emblem of national
sovereignty. Our own country stamps its purest gold coin with the
likeness of this king of birds and calls the coin itself an Eagle. Such
honor is granted because no other bird of the air and no beast of the
field was ever so graceful, so swift, or so aggressive; there is no eye so
keen, no talon so sharp or powerful. When an Eagle screams, all beasts
seek cover, and man himself is awed. An Eagle is also independent and
takes no food except that provided by his own power and skill. Furthermore, no other was ever so loyal to its kind. An Eagle will die in defense
of its nest.

The rapid rise of this college from comparative obscurity to a
place among the great educational institutions of the State of Texas
has not been unlike the rise of an Eagle from the valley to a place on
the mountain top. Our faculty, our students, and our alumni will
never be satisfied until they see our college resting on the topmost
peak of fame.

Since February 1, 1922, Eagles, to the supporters of the dear old
green and white, has had an additional significance. It suggests that
esteem and loyalty for school, and of school for team, which is so
characteristic of the N. T. S. N. C. The keen eye, the speed and endur-
ance, the aggressiveness, the beauty, the strength, and the independence
of the Eagle typify similar qualities found in our teams and in our
school.

"SCREAM, EAGLES, SCREAM!" And such a volume of sound would burst forth from the throats of hundreds of loyal rooters that the roof of the gymnasium would almost be lifted. No team is able to win games without the proper support from the sidelines, and many victories are won by the rooters on the sidelines who are backing the team on the basket ball court.

Rooters and yell leader deserve their share of praise in bringing the 1922 T. I. A. A. basket ball championship to the North Texas State Normal College. "SCREAM, EAGLES, SCREAM!"

Trophies Won in 1922

THE T. I. A. A. TROPHY   THE A. A. U. TROPHY

Hot Dog! Best Old Team in Texas

If the Eagle basket ball team beat the Southwestern University team it was almost sure that the Eagles could win the T. I. A. A. championship without difficulty. When the news reached Denton that the fast Southwestern team had been defeated the second time by the Eagles, it was planned by loyal rooters to celebrate this occasion. A large bonfire was built in the middle of a street near the College, and merrymaking was carried on until about 3 o'clock the next morning.

It was planned to meet the victorious team the next morning when it arrived on the 9:18 train from Georgetown. Many students marched to the railroad station through mud, rain, and sleet, and such a demonstration had never been given to a Normal team as was given to the victorious Eagles. The members of the team and coach St. Clair were carried from the train to waiting automobiles and escorted by the students to the college campus amid shouts of joy and triumph. HOT DOG!

The Student-Faculty Council

THE Student-Faculty Council was originally a body created to revise the regulations governing the school. The student members were elected by the students, one from each college class being chosen to represent his class, and one from the Normal School being chosen to represent that group; and the faculty members were appointed by the president. After the work of revising the régulations was over, the president retained the Council as part of the organization of the school. He also retained the ten original members for the year, and enlarged the body by adding one faculty member and one student.

The Council is a legislative body. It is primarily interested in passing such legislation as will protect the students and help the best interests of the school. While laws governing discipline are the subjects of much of its deliberation, these are not all it gives its time to. It is ready to help any committee with its individual problems by giving counsel, by making recommendations to proper authorities, or by passing regulations. Because of its newness, the Council has felt its way carefully, and has tried to be constructive and at the same time conservative. It is the policy of the Council not to interfere with the work of existing committees.

The ultimate good resulting from the work of the Council, however, is not to be found in a code of laws, however worthy such a code may be; it is to be found in the closer co-operation between students and faculty, and in the warmer sympathy arising between the two groups, because of the work in common done by them for a common cause. Such a community of interests can not fail in bringing about a heartier sympathy and a clearer understanding, and must result in a college life that is higher in tone, purer in color, closer in harmony, and richer in culture than a college life can be where discord or jealousies abound.

Though the work so far has not been spectacular nor revolutionary, yet the Council modestly claims to have helped somewhat toward raising the standards of scholarship and toward democratizing the school. It is a body of earnest men and women who want to serve their school well, and who want to leave for their successors a reputation for clear thinking and honest action.

In Memoriam

JEFFERSON NEWBY SIMMONS, A. B., A. M.
April 2nd, 1883—May 14th, 1921.

J. N. Simmons

MR. J. N. SIMMONS matriculated as a student in the North Texas State Normal College on April 21, 1909. He remained in school the remainder of the session of 1908-09 and during the session 1909-10. He was a student also during the summer terms of 1909 and 1910 and graduated with the class in May, 1911.

After graduating here he was a teacher at Josephine, Texas, one year, 1910-11. The next year he accepted the superintendency of the Navajo Industrial School, maintained by the Methodist Church of the Indians at Farmington, New Mexico.

Before the close of the session the buildings of this school were literally swept away by a flood. Mr. Simmons had succeeded, before the main crest of the flood reached the school, in sending to a place of safety all the pupils and all the corps of teachers except one teacher and himself, who remained in the buildings. The teacher who remained with him was drowned and Mr. Simmons himself narrowly escaped, being forced to remain in the swollen and turbulent stream thirty-six hours. The next year Mr. Simmons devoted his time to traveling and lecturing in the Northwest and Northeast for the purpose of raising funds with which to rebuild the institution. He succeeded in his undertaking and the school was rebuilt in a place of safety and given vastly improved quarters.

From 1913 to the time he came as a member of the Faculty here, he was either teaching in the states of Indiana and New York or attending college.

He received the degree A. B. from De Pauw University in 1918 and A. M. from Teachers College, Columbia University, in 1920. In both these institutions he majored in Education.

He began his work as a member of this faculty in the capacity of Director of the Training School in February, 1920, which place he held till his death in May, 1921.

Mr. Simmons was painstaking as a teacher, an industrious worker, an exact scholar, conscientious in the performance of every duty and faithful to every trust ever imposed upon him. He was highly esteemed by faculty and students and he was best liked and appreciated by those who knew him most intimately.

YUCCA PLANT

ADMINISTRATION BUILDING

LIBRARY AND SCIENCE BUILDING

WHERE THE FLOWERS BLOOM

IN THE SHADE

HEART OF THE CAMPUS

CAMPUS FOLIAGE

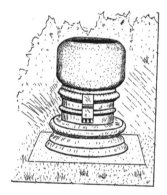

Twenty-three

SCIENCE BUILDING

HEATING PLANT

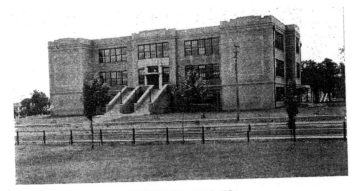

EDUCATION BUILDING

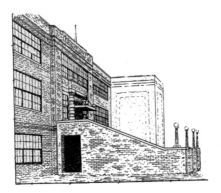

MANUAL ARTS' BUILDING

ROSE COVERED FOUNTAIN

LIBRARY

READING ROOM—LIBRARY

DINING ROOM—MANUAL ARTS

WEST GATE

ADMINISTRATION

Hon. A.C. Goeth, Pres.

Hon. R.J. Eckhardt

Hon. M.O. Flowers, V.-Pres.

Hon. J.J. Bennett

Hon. A.B. Watkins

Miss Margie E. Neal

BOARD OF REGENTS

WILLIAM HERSCHEL BRUCE, A. M., Ph. D., LL. D.
President

PRESIDENT BRUCE AND MRS. BRUCE

CAMPUS FOLIAGE AROUND PRESIDENT'S HOME

Miss Ruby C. Smith, A. B., A. M., Associate Dean of Women . . . . *Spanish*
Miss Edith L. Clark, B. Lit., A. M., Dean of Women . . . . . *English*
W. D. Butler, A. B., A. M., Dean . . . . *Mathematics*
E. D. Criddle, B. Lit., Associate Dean . . . . *History*

S. B. Neff, A. B., A. M., Ph. D. . . . . *English*
Miss Myrtle C. Brown, A. B., A. M. . . . . *Mathematics*
Miss Lillian M. Parrill . . . . *Music*
Hugh Porter, A. B., A. M. . . . . *Mathematics*

A. O. CALHOUN, B. S. . . . . *Chemistry*
J. W. PENDER, A. B. . . . . *Government*
J. N. BROWN, A. B., A. M. . . . . *Latin*
S. A. BLACKBURN, B. E. . . . . *Manual Training*

MRS. PHOEBE GOODE MIZZELL . . . . *Critic Teacher*
MISS MAMIE E. SMITH . . . . *Music and Critic Teacher*
MISS KATHERINE HORNBEAK, A. B., A. M. . . . . . *English*
B. B. HARRIS, B. S. . . . . *Agriculture*

Miss Bessie L. Shook, A. B., A. M. . . . . English
Mrs. Grace R. West, B. S. . . . . Science
Miss Mignonette Spillman, A. B., A. M. . . . . Latin
Mrs. Eleanor H. Gibbs . . . . Drawing

A. S. Keith . . . . Principal Training School
Miss Julia McIntyre, B. S. . . . . Critic Teacher
Mrs. Earl Morrow . . . . Piano
R. L. Turner, B. S. . . . . Physics

F. V. GARRISON, B. S. . . . . *Education*
MISS LENA M. CHARTER, A. M. . . . . *Home Ecomonics*
MISS D. MARIE STOREY, B. S. . . . . *Home Economics*
T. E. PETERS, A. B., A. M. *Mathematics*

MISS ELIZABETH A. HILLYAR . . . . *Drawing*
L. L. MILLER, A. M. . . . . *Physics*
MISS CORALEE GARRISON, A. B. . . . . *Reading*
MISS MARGARET LOUISE WHITE . . . . *Critic Teacher*

E. H. Farrington, A. B. . . . . *Agriculture*
Miss Edna St. John, B. S. . . . . *Home Economics*
Miss Beulah Anna Harriss, A. B. . . . . *Physical Education*
J. W. Beatty, A. M. . . . . *Education*

S. S. McKay, A. B., A. M. . . . . *History*
Miss Ellie Virginia Broadfoot, A. B. . . . . . . *Physical Education*
Mrs. Hixie Pittman Ellison . . . . *Librarian*
J. P. Downer, A. B. . . . . *Mathematics*

L. W. Newton, A. B., A. M. . . . . *History*
Miss Effie Collier, A. B. . . . . *Critic Teacher*
Miss Clara Edith Morley, A. B., A. M. . . . . *English*
Miss Myrtle E. Williams, A. B., A. M. . . . . *English*

L. P. Floyd, B. S. . . . . *Chemistry*
Miss Marie Emma Phillips, A. M. . . . . *English*
Mrs. Frankie Lain Compton . . . . *Critic Teacher*
B. E. Looney, A. B., A. M. . . . . *English*

Miss Pearl Artena Cross, B. S.   Home Economics
A. A. Miller, LL. B.   Commerce
G. M. Crutsinger, A. M.   Biology
W. W. Wright   Bookkeeper

J. H, Legett
Mrs. Pearl C. McCracken   Agriculture
C. M. Mizzell, B. S.   Librarian
J. R. Swenson, A. B., A. M.   Critic Teacher
                                               Education and Geography

Ross Compton, A. B., B. S. . . . . *History*
Miss Lillian Obera Walker . . . . *Librarian*
Miss Ruth L. Parker, B. L. I. . . . . *Reading*
T. J. Fouts, A. B. . . . . *Physical Education*

E. L. Anderson, A. B. . . . . *French*
Miss Mary C. Sweet, A. B., A. M. . . . . *English*
Mrs. Cora M. Martin, B. S. . . . . *Education*
J. W. Smith . . . . *Secretary-Treasurer*

J. W. St. Clair, A. B. . . . . *Physical Education*
Miss Lucile O. Page, B. L. I. . . . . *Reading*
Mrs. Lee Etta Nelson, A. B. . . . . *History and English*
W. J. McConnell, A. B., A. M. . . . . *Economics*

Mrs. Jack Johnson, A. B. . . . . *English*
Miss Virginia Haile . . . . *Critic Teacher*
Miss Mary Anderson, B. Mus. . . . . *Piano*
Miss Anna Irion Powell, A. B. . . . . *History*

G. A. ODAM, A. M. . . . . *Education and Director of Training School*
MISS CORA BELLE WILSON, A. M. . . . . *History*
A. C. McGINNIS . . . . *Commerce*
P. E. McDONALD . . . . *Registrar*

J. N. BIGBEE, A. B. . . . . *Education*
W. P. BOYD . . . . *Secretary to President*
W. T. DOGGETT, A. M. . . . . *Education*
DONALD McDONALD, A. M. . . . . *History*

J. E. BLAIR, B. S. . . . . *Education*
MISS JANIE PRICHARD DUGGAN, A. M. . . . . *Education*
MISS OLIVE HALBERT, PH. B. . . . . *Assistant Librarian*
J. F. PEELER, B. S. . . . . *Mathematics*

H. J. P. VITZ, B. S. . . . . *Manual Training*
MISS EVALINA HARRINGTON, B. S., A. B. . . . . *Education*
MISS MARIE ELIZABETH RUSS, A. B. . . . . *Student Life Secretary*
W. N. MASTERS, B. S., A. B. . . . . *Chemistry*

E. G. GRAFTON, A. B. . . . . *Geography*
CHARLES C. DAVIE . . . . *Assistant Registrar*
J. SHIRLEY HODGES . . . . *Laboratory Assistant*
C. A. BRIDGES, A. B. . . . . *History and English*

MRS. ELIZABETH McNEW WINTER, B. S. . . . . *Home Economics*
J. P. GLASGOW, A. B., A. M. . . . . *Biology*
G. G. HERREN, A. B., A. M. . . . . *English*
MISS INEZ McCRACKEN . . . . *Drawing*

Miss Maymie Patrick . . . . *Critic Teacher*
F. W. Emerson, A. M. . . . . *English*
C. H. Dillehay, A. M. . . . . *Mathematics*
Miss Mary Bell Myers, A. B. . . . . *Critic Teacher*

B. H. Miller, A. B. . . . . *History*
W. L. Willis . . . . *Mathematics*
Julius Dorsey, A. M. . . . . *History*
L. F. Connell . . . . *Geography*

Miss Cora Elder Stafford, B. S. . . . . *Drawing*
Miss Valerie Reeves . . . . *Music*
Miss Sallie M. Pinckney, A. B. . . . . . *Student Life Sec'y*

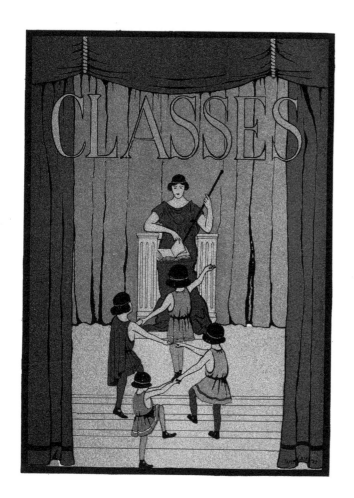

Our Student Ex-Members of the Texas Legislature

J. L. YARBROUGH, of Ponder, Junior Class,
Member of THIRTY-SECOND AND THIRTY-THIRD LEGISLATURES,
Representative from Collin County.

P. M. JOHNSTON, of Valley View, Sophomore Class,
Member of THIRTY-FIRST AND THIRTY-SECOND LEGISLATURES,
Representative from Parker County.

J. W. STANFORD, of Martins Mill, Senior Class,
Member of THIRTY-FOURTH LEGISLATURE,
Representative from Van Zandt County.

Class Officers, 1921-22

SENIOR CLASS

RALPH PATRICK . . . . *President*
MAYDELL WALLACE . . . . *Secretary-Treasurer*
BERTHA STOCKARD . . . . *Campus Chat Reporter*
R. H. DAVIS . . . . *Student Council Representative*

JUNIOR CLASS

HOMER WEEKS . . . . *President*
ESSIE BALL . . . . *Vice-President*
ILENE COMPTON . . . . *Secretary-Treasurer*
HELEN EMBERSON . . . . *Campus Chat Reporter*
WESTON L. MURRAY . . . . . *Student Council Representative*

SOPHOMORE CLASS

BEN ROBERTS . . . . *President*
CLYDE COOPER . . . . *Vice-President*
VARUE ORNDORFF . . . . *Secretary-Treasurer*
J. B. DRAKE . . . . *Campus Chat Reporter*
W. C. BLANKENSHIP . . . . . *Student Council Representative*

FRESHMAN CLASS

DAN MCALLISTER . . . . *President*
RUTH CRAWFORD . . . . *Secretary-Treasurer*
CLARENCE B. JOHNSTON . . . . . . *Campus Chat Reporter*
J. C. MCDONALD . . . . . . *Student Council Representative*

SECOND YEAR CLASS

CARROLL WILSON . . . . *President*
F. A. COFFEE . . . . *Vice-President*
GLADYS NORMAND . . . . *Secretary-Treasurer*
BILL PATTERSON . . . . *Campus Chat Reporter*
ONAS BROWN . . . . *Student Council Representative*

FIRST YEAR CLASS

JIM POWELL . . . . *President*
FRANK DEUPREE . . . . *Vice-President*
ANNIE MAE PATTERSON . . . . *Secretary-Treasurer*
E. C. HATTEN . . . . *Campus Chat Reporter*

SENIOR

Seniors

Mary Sophia Bauer, A. B. . . *Tioga*
  Y. W. C. A., 1922; Education Exchange,
1922; C. L. C., Delegate to City Federation, 1922.

Mrs. S. A. Blackburn, B. S. . *Denton*

Mrs. Ilene Hodges Compton, B. S.
  . . . . . *Denton*
  Y. W. C. A., 1922; Education Exchange,
1922; Dramatic Club, Secretary-Treasurer, 1922; Choral Club, 1922·

Seniors

ROBERT H. DAVIS, A. B. .   .   *Thalia*

Representative of Senior Class on Students Council, 1922; Education Exchange, 1922; Dramatic Club, 1922; Reagan Literary Society, 1920-'21; Campus Chat Reporter, 1922; Silver Striper Club, 1922; Students Council, Chairman of Students Section, 1922; Publications Council, 1922; Press Club, Vice-President, 1922; Boys Glee Club, 1922; The Scribes, Vice-President, 1921.

LILLIE DILL, B. S. .   .   .   *Rosston*

CLIFTON C. DOAK, B. S. .   .   *Denton*

Y. M. C. A., 1922; Education Exchange, 1922; Dramatic Club, 1922; Reagan Literary Society, President, 1921; Silver Striper Club, President, 1921; Discipline Committee, 1922; Athletic Council, President, 1922; Press Club, 1922; The Scribes, 1921; Associate Editor of 1922 Yucca.

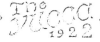

1922

PAUL DOUGLASS, B. S. . . . *Denton*

Lee Literary Society; Basket Ball, 1918, 1919, 1920; President Physical Education Club, Summer, 1921; President Denton County Club, Summer, 1921; Band, 1918, 1919; Silver Striper Club, Summer, 1921.

INEZ EVANS, A. B. . . . *Nevada*

HAZEL FLOYD, A. B. . . *Denton*

Y. W. C. A., 1918, 1919; Mary Arden Club, 1919, 1920, 1921; Denton County Club, 1918, 1919, 1920, 1921; Press Club, Secretary, 1919, 1921; Choral Club, 1918; Athletic Association, 1920, 1921; Arts and Crafts Club, 1920, President, 1921; Vice-President of Junior Class, 1921; Representative of Junior IV Class, 1919; Secretary-Treasurer of Senior Class, Summer, 1921; Campus Chat Staff, Summer, 1921; Art Editor of 1921 Yucca.

LESTER LEE ROY FRITZ, B. S. *McKinney*
Y. M. C. A., Cabinet Member, 1919, 1921; Education Exchange, 1922; Reagan Literary Society, 1919, 1920, 1921; Sergeant-at-Arms, 1922; Henry W. Grady Literary Society, Summer, 1920; Collin County Club, 1920, 1921, 1922; Silver Striper Club, 1922; Intersociety Debater, 1922.

H. TRACY HAYES, B. S. . . *Gustine*.
Education Exchange, 1922; Lee Literary Society, 1919, 1921, 1922; Comanche County Club, Summer, 1919, 1921; Silver Striper Club, President, 1922; Choral Club, Secretary, 1922.

FRED C. HUGHES, A. B. . . . *Center*
President Sophomore Class, 1921; Education Exchange, 1922; Lee Literary Society, Critic and Secretary, 1921, President, 1922; Dramatic Club, Vice-President, 1921; Henry W. Grady Literary Society, Summer, 1920; A. E. F. Club, Campus Chat Reporter, 1921, 1922; Shelby County Club, President, 1920; Publications Council, 1921, 1922; El Circulo Espanol, 1921, 1922; Press Club, President, 1921, 1922; Choral Club, 1917, 1921; Boys' Glee Club, 1922; Inter-Collegiate Debater, 1921; Inter-Society Debater, 1922; Editor-in-Chief of Campus Chat, 1922.

VERA JOBE, B. S.   .   .   .   *Gorman*

W. M. V. LEMENS, A. B. .   . *Rainbow*

Y. M. C. A., President, 1922; Education Exchange, 1922; Lee Literary Society, 1921, Vice-President, 1922; Oratorical Association, 1918; "Five Tribes" County Club, Pres., 1918; Silver Striper, Reporter, S. S., 1921; French Club, 1918; Press Club, 1922; Choral Club, 1918; The Scribes; Intercollegiate Debater, 1922; K. O. E., 1922.

BERTA MAY LOONEY, B. S. .   *Denton*

Y. W. C. A., Cabinet Member, 1922; Mary Arden, 1918-1922; Press Club, 1922; Girls Glee Club, 1919, '20 '22; Choral Club, 1922; Associate Editor of Campus Chat, 1922; Life Service Band, President, 1922; Student Volunteer Band, 1922.

MERICK DAVIS McGAUGHEY, A. B., *Vera*

Class Artist, Junior Class, 1922; Y. M.
C. A., Cabinet Member, 1920, 1922;
Education Exchange, 1922; Lee Literary
Society, 1920 Chaplain, 1922; West
Texas Club, Summer, 1921.

EVA MONTGOMERY, B. S. .   *Galveston*
    Y. W. C. A.

MRS. MILDRED MONTGOMERY, B. S.
    .   .   .   . *Denton*

Seniors

D. H. NORRIS, A. B. . . *Kingsland*

Lee Literary Society, President, 1915; South Texas Club, 1914; Central Texas Club; Athletic Club, 1915.

WILLIE H. NUTT, A. B., *Addington, Okla.*

RALPH CURTIS PATRICK, A. B. . *Denton*

President Senior Class, 1922; Y. M. C. A., Cabinet Member, 1922; Education Exchange, 1922; Dramatic Club, 1920, 1922; Reagan Literary Society, 1919, 1922; Silver Striper Club, 1922; Publications Council, 1922; Associate Editor of Campus Chat, Summer, 1921.

LEIGH PECK, A. B. . . . . *Denton*

Secretary of Senior Class, 1922; Secretary of Second Year Class, 1919; Education Exchange, President, 1922; Current Literature Club, 1922; Mary Arden Club, 1922; French Club, 1921, 1922; Executive Council of Education Exchange, 1922.

JOHNNIE M. ROADY, B. S. . *Denton*

Y. M. C. A., 1918, 1919; Lee Literary Society, 1918, 1919; Dramatic Club, 1922; Collin County Club, Summer, 1919, 1920, 1921; Denton County Club, Summer, 1919, 1920, 1921; Track, 1922; Education Exchange, 1922; Fine Arts Club, 1922.

MRS. LULU K. SHUMAKER, A. B. . *Dallas*

Y. W. C. A., 1922; Education Exchange, Secretary, 1922; Choral Club, President, 1922.

Seniors

BERTHA STOCKARD, B. S. . . *Garza*

Representative of Senior Class, 1922; Y. W. C. A., 1918, 1920, Cabinet Member, 1922; Current Literature Club, 1919; Physical Education Club, 1920, 1922; Publications Council, 1922; Press Club, 1922; Choral Club, 1920.

BLANCHE MAYDELL WALLACE, B. S.
. . . . . . *Pilot Point*

Vice-President of Senior Class, 1922; Y. W. C. A., Cabinet Member, 1918, 1920; Education Exchange, 1922; Current Literature Club, Vice-President, 1918, President, 1919; Denton County Club, 1920, 1921; Students Council, Secretary, 1922; Publications Council, 1922; Press Club, 1922; Physical Education Club, 1922.

HOMER WEEKS, B. S. . . *Wolfe City*

Y. M. C. A., 1914; Education Exchange, Summer, 1921; Lee Literary Society, 1919, 1922; Fannin County Club, Summer, 1919, 1921; Silver Striper Club, 1922; Choral Club, 1922; Boys Glee Club, 1922; Physical Education Club, 1922.

Seniors

CARL R. YOUNG, B. S. . . *Fort Worth*

Lee Literary Society, 1921, 1922; Dramatic Club, 1921, President, 1922; A. E. F. Club, 1920, 1921, Vice-President, 1922; Tarrant County Club, Summer Sessions, 1920, 1921; Chapel Committee, 1922; Publications Council, 1922; Press Club, 1921, 1922; Choral Club, 1922; Assistant Business Manager of Publications, 1921; General Art of 1921 Yucca; Editor-In-Chief of 1922 Yucca.

ELIZABETH EARLE ADAMS, A. B., *Crockett*

Y. W. C. A., 1922; Mary Arden Club, Campus Chat Reporter, 1922; Press Club, 1922.

REBECCA MAE JOHNSTON, B. S. . *Denton*

Y. W. C. A., 1922; Education Exchange, 1922; Mary Arden Club, 1922.

The Senior Speaks

Alone within the silence of my room,
Beneath a pale, dejected light,
I try in vain to pierce the verbal gloom
That shrouds the fate of Cressida from sight.
Upon a table top, in bookish guise,
Five goblins range themselves as on a throne,
My sovereigns they, directing weary eyes
And mind to knowledge I would fain postpone.
How could I bear the labors of the night
But for the thought that on the morrow's dawn
I may with you parade the walks in sight
Of all my friends upon the College lawn?
Accept, dear heart, these lines, if you will deign,
Honoring you, my loved, my trusted cane.

L. P.

JUNIOR

Juniors

RUBY ADAMS..............*Denton*	FRITZ HUMPHREYS........*Denton*
J. S. ANDERSON...........*Grand Saline*	INEZ JONES................*Denton*
GLEN BALCH..............*Venus*	OTA BELL MCCAIN........*Fort Worth*
C. L. CALDWELL...........*Princeton*	W. L. MURRAY...........*San Saba*
CLARA COX................*Celina*	JEWELL MURRELL..........*Gatesville*
HELEN EMBERSON..........*Pilot Point*	OPAL TRUSSELL............*Boyd*
EUGENIA HENDERSON.......*Okemah, Okla.*	GEORGIA WATSON..........*Venus*

ELVERA DALE WEBB.......*Nevada*

SOPHOMORE

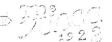

LELA QUAY ADAMS . . .. *Denton*
  Y. W. C. A., 1921, 1922; Education
Exchange, 1921, 1922; Denton County
Club, Summer, 1921.

S. D. ADAMS . . . . . . *Denton*
  Education Exchange, 1922; Lee Liter-
ary Society, 1922; Dramatic Club, 1922;
Band.

SIDNEY J. ADAMS . . . . . *Holland*
  Lee Literary Society, 1922.

E. M. ALLGOOD . . . . . *Denton*
  Y. M. C. A., 1922; Education Ex-
change, 1922; Lee Literary Society, 1919;
Press Club, 1918, 1919.

FINIS ALLRED . . ´ . . . *Hillsboro*
  Y. W. C. A., 1922; Education Ex-
change, 1922; C. L. C., 1922; Dramatic
Club, 1922; Hill County Club, 1921.

ETHEL ANDREWS . . . . *Fort Worth*

ANNIE FAYE ANDREWS . . *McKinney*
  Y. W. C. A., 1922; Education Exchange, 1922; Mary Arden, 1922.

ESTELLE AUSTIN . . . .. *Harrold*

Sophomores

GRACE BECK . . . . . *Wills Point*

Education Exchange, 1922; C. L. C., 1922; Van Zandt County Club, 1922; Physical Education Club, 1922.

ETHELYNE BENTLEY . . . *Trinidad*

W. C. BLANKENSHIP . . . *Ovalo*

Representative of Sophomore Class to Students' Council, 1922; Y. M. C. A., Campus Chat Reporter, 1921, 1922; Education Exchange, 1922; Dramatic Club, Summer, 1918; Reagan Literary Society, President, 1920, 1921, 1922; Hill County Club, President, Summer, 1918; Faculty-Students' Council, President, 1922; Press Club, 1922; Choral Club, 1922; Boys' Glee Club, 1922; Inter-Society Debater, 1917; Inter-Collegiate Debater, 1921, 1922.

LOUISE BOOKER . . . . . . *Denton*

WILLIE PEARL BRASHEARS . . *Denton*

Y. W. C. A., 1922; Education Exchange, 1922; Girls' Glee Club, 1922.

MABLE B. BROWN . . *Blooming Grove*

ETHEL BUNCH . . . . . . *Powell*

Y. W. C. A., 1921, 1922; Mary Arden, 1921, Vice-President, 1922; Dramatic Club, 1921; Campus Chat Reporter, 1922; Navarro County Club, 1919; Press Club, 1922; College Life Editor of Yucca, 1922.

GRACE CALDWELL . . *Sulphur Springs*

Y. W. C. A., 1922; Education Exchange, 1922; C. L. C., Treasurer, 1922; Kindergarten Primary Club, 1922.

Sophomores

MARY EMILY CARLISLE . . *McKinney*
Y. W. C. A., 1921, 1922; Education
Exchange, 1922; Mary Arden Club, 1921,
1922; Collin County Club, 1921.

ENIE BESS CARLTON . . *Anson*
Y. W. C. A., Treasurer, 1921, 1922; Current
Literature Club, Treasurer, 1920, 1921; West
Texas County Club, 1921.

HENRYETTA CARTER . . *Edgewood*
Y. W. C. A., 1921, 1922; Dramatic Club,
1922; Physical Education Club, 1922.

JESSIE L CATES . . . *Crowell*
Y. W. C. A., 1922; Education Exchange,
1922; Mary Arden Club, 1922; Dramatic
Club, 1922.

EULA MAE CAUGHRAN . . *Chisholm*
Y. W. C. A., 1922.

RUBYLEA CLEMENT . . *Denton*
Education Exchange, 1922; Basket Ball,
1922.

MRS. EUGENE COOK . . *Denton*
Y. W. C. A., 1917, 1918, 1922; Denton
County Club, 1922; Good House Keepers'
Club, President, 1922.

ANNIE COOPER . . *Durant, Miss.*
Y. W. C. A., 1922; Education Exchange,
1922; Mary Arden Club, Campus Chat
Representative, 1922.

Sophomores

C. L. COOPER . . . . . . *Denton*

Vice-President of Sophomore Class, 1922; Y. M. C. A., 1921, 1922; Education Exchange, 1922; Lee Literary Society, 1920, 1921, 1922; Athletic Council, Student Manager, 1922; Boys' Glee Club, 1920; Track, 1921.

ETHEL COOPER . . . *Durant, Miss.*

Y. W. C. A., 1922; Education Exchange, 1922; C. L. C., 1922.

E. M. CONNELL . . . . . · *Denton*

Y. M. C. A., Secretary, 1921, President, 1922; Education Exchange, 1922; Lee Literary Society, Secretary, 1921, 1922; East Texas Club, President, 1921; Silver Striper Club, Secretary, 1921, 1922.

CONWAY CRIDER . . . . . *Bonham*

Y. W. C. A., 1922; Education Exchange, 1922; C. L. C., Treasurer, 1922.

MARY JOE CRESWELL . . . *Aubrey*

PAULINE CURRY . . . . *Granbury*

Education Exchange, 1922; Mary Arden, 1922; Publications Council, 1922; Press Club, 1922; Choral Club, 1922.

C. A. DAVIS . . . . . . *Thalia*

Education Exchange, 1922; Reagan Literary Society, President, 1921, 1922; A. E. F. Club, 1921; Campus Chat Reporter, 1922; West Texas Club, President, Summer, 1921; Press Club, 1922; Boys' Glee Club, 1922.

DIXIE DEAN . . . . . . *Detroit*

Sophomores

ALICE DeSHIELDS . . . *McKinney*

RUBY GRACE DICKSON . . . *Frost*
Y. W. C. A., 1921, 1922; Education Exchange, 1922; Dramatic Club, 1921, 1922; Navarro County Club, 1921; Press Club, 1922; Typist of Yucca, 1922.

UNA E. DOUGLASS . . . . *Denton*

J. B. DRAKE . . . . . . *Denton*

EMMA BELL BRAKE . . . *Richardson*
Education Exchange, 1922.

IRENE DUNCAN . . . . . *Bartlett*
Y. W. C. A., 1921, 1922; Education Exchange, 1922; Mary Arden, 1921, 1922; Band, 1921; Arts and Crafts Club, 1921.

VIRGINIA DUNN . . . *Ben Wheeler*
Y. W. C. A., Education Exchange, 1922; Current Literature Club, 1921, 1922; Van Zandt County Club, 1921, 1922.

RUSSEL E. EDWARDS . . *Westminster*

Sophomores

LILLIAN ELDER . . . . *Pilot Point*
Y. W. C. A., Chairman of Poster Committee, 1922; Education Exchange, 1922; Current Literature Club, 1922.

N. D. GEDDIE . . . . . . *Canton*

RUTH GRAY . . . . . *Denton*

JENNIE GREEN . . . . . *Weimar*

OLA BESS GRIFFIS . . . . . *Italy*
Y. W. C. A.; Current Literature Club, Vice-President, 1920, 1921; Ellis County Club, 1921.

LIZZIE GRIZZARD . . . *Honey Grove*
Y. W. C. A., 1921, 1922; Choral Club, 1922.

EMILY HAYS . . . . . *New Boston*

VELMA HILL . . . . . . *Hubbard*
Y. W. C. A., 1920, 1921, 1922; Education Exchange, 1922; Dramatic Club, 1922; Navarro County Club, 1921.

Sophomores

GLADYS HINES . *Mesilla, New Mexico*

EDNA HOLLOMAN . . . *McKinney*
Y. W. C. A., 1922.

LULU HOPPER . . . . . *Denton*

VIVIAN HUFFAKER . . . . . *Denton*
Y. W. C. A., Chairman of Music Committee; Education Exchange, 1922; Mary Arden Club, 1922; Girls' Glee Club, 1922; Choral Club, Accompanist, 1922; Boys' Glee Club, Accompanist, 1922.

PEARL JANUARY . . . . . *Denton*

HERBERT JARNAGIN . . . . *Denton*
Lee Literary Society, 1922; A. E. F. Club, 1922.

EMMA JEWELL JASPER . . . *Dallas*
Y. W. C. A., 1922; Education Exchange, 1922; Mary Arden Club, 1922.

JOELLA JEMIMA JENKINS . *Clarksville*
Y. W. C. A., Reporter, 1921, 1922; Current Literature Club, Treasurer, 1921; Red River County Club, 1921; Press Club, 1922; Scribes, 1921.

Sophomores

LAVERNE JONES . . . *Valley Mills*
Y. W. C. A., 1921, 1922; Education
Exchange, 1922.

LENA MARTIN . . . . . . *Jason*

EDITH MARTIN . . . . *Fort Worth*
Dramatic Club, 1922; Press Club, 1922;
Yucca Art Editor, 1922; Kindergarten
Primary Club, 1922.

LILLIAN MASSENGILL .. . *Terrell*
Y. W. C. A., 1922; Education Exchange,
1922; Current Literature Club, President,
1922; Kaufman County Club, 1921;
Choral Club, 1921; Scribes, 1915; C. L. C.
Delegate to City Federation; 1915.

LEONARD K. MAXCY . . . *Denton*
Y. M. C. A., 1922; Lee Literary Society,
1922; Athletic Council, Assistant Business
Manager, 1922.

DAN MCALISTER . . . . . *Venus*
President of Freshman Class, 1921; Lee
Literary Society, 1921, 1922; Press Club,
1922; Football, 1919, 1920, 1921; Basket
Ball, 1921, 1922; Baseball, 1921; Athletic
Editor of Yucca, 1922; President of Physi-
cal Education Club, 1922.

BERT MCDUFF . . . . . *Lillian*

LEE MCGLOTHLIN . . . . *Lamkin*
Education Exchange, 1922; Current
Literature Club, 1922; Physical Education
Club, 1922.

Sophomores

EFFIE ELIZABETH McLEOD . *Florence*

Y. W. C. A., 1916, 1920, 1922; Education Exchange, 1922; C. L. C., 1922; Williamson County Club, Secretary, 1920.

EXA MINTER . . . . . . *Como*

Mary Arden Club, 1922; Fine Arts Club, Secretary-Treasurer, 1922; Press Club, 1922; Art Editor of Yucca, 1922.

ELMA NAUGLE . . . . . *Prosper*

Y. W. C. A., 1922; Education Exchange, 1922; Girls' Glee Club, 1922.

VARUE ORNDORFF . . . . *Gordon*

Secretary of Sophomore Class, 1922; Y. W. C. A., 1921; Mary Arden Club, 1922; Dramatic Club, 1921, 1922; Choral Club, 1921; Education Exchange, 1922,

INA M. OWENS . . . . . . *Ennis*

Y. W. C. A., 1920, 1921, 1922; Mary Arden Club, 1922; Ellis County Club, 1921; Athletic Council, Secretary-Treasurer, 1922; Girls' Basket Ball Team, Captain, 1922; Physical Education Club, 1920, Secretary-Treasurer, 1922.

RUTH PARKER . . . . *Santa Anna*

Y. W. C. A., 1922; Education Exchange, 1922; Mary Arden Club, 1922.

HARRY LEE PINKERTON . *Ben Wheeler*

Reagan Literary Society, 1921, 1922; Boys' Glee Club, 1922; Basket Ball, 1921, Captain, 1922; Physical Education Club, 1922.

RUBY POWER . . . *Archer City*

Y. W. C. A., 1922.

Sophomores

LOUISE PRESTON . . . . *Denton*

Y. W. C. A., 1922; Dramatic Club, 1922; Denton County Club, 1922; Girls' Glee Club, 1922; Basket Ball, 1922; Physical Education Club, 1922.

LORENA PRUNTY . . . . . *Denton*

J. E. PURVIS . . . . . . *Proctor*

PEARL RAGLE . . . . . . *Dicey*

Y. W. C. A., 1921, 1922; Education Exchange, 1922; Current Literature Club, Sergeant-at-Arms, 1922.

RALPH RAMEY . . . . . *Denton*

LUCILE RANGELEY . . . *Hillsboro*

Y. W. C. A., 1922; Education Exchange, 1922.

BEN H. ROBERTS . . . . *Denton*

President of Sophomore Class, 1922; Dramatic Club, 1922; Reagan Literary Society, 1922; Silver Striper, 1922; Press Club, 1922; Boys' Glee Club, Chat Reporter, 1922.

PAT NEFF ROBERTS . . . . *Denton*

Representative of Freshman Class on Yucca Staff, 1921; Associate Editor of Campus Chat, 1921.

Sophomores

RAYMOND SCHULZE . . . . . *Denton*

BESS SHOTWELL . . . . . *Denton*

ALMA SIMS . . . . *Denton*
 Y. W. C. A., 1921, 1922; Education
Exchange, 1922; Mary Arden Club, 1922;
Denton County Club, 1921; Fine Arts
Club, 1922.

JULIA STAFFORD . . . . . . *Alice*

LILLIAN SLOAN . . . . . . *Dublin*
 Y. W. C. A., 1922; Education Exchange,
1922; Current Literature Club, 1922; Erath
County Club, 1921; Choral Club, 1922.

MATTIE SMITH . . . . . . *Vernon*
 Y. W. C. A., 1922; Education Ex-
change, 1922; Current Literature Club,
Vice-President, 1921, Secretary, 1921;
West Texas Club, 1921; Choral Club,
1922.

A. D. STARLING . . . . . *Grapevine*

LOUISE STOUT . . . . . . *Denton*
 Y. W. C. A., 1922; Dramatic Club, 1922;
Mary Arden Club, 1922.

Sophomores

ALICE STRICKLAND . . . . *Cisco*

Y. W. C. A., 1922; Education Exchange, 1922; Kindergarten Primary Club, 1922.

LULU SULLIVAN . . . . . *Garner*

Y. W. C. A., 1922; Education Exchange, 1922; Mary Arden Club, 1922.

LEON TALIAFERRO . . . . *Denton*

Education Exchange, 1922; Press Club, 1922; Class Representative for Freshman; on the Campus Chat, 1919; Yucca Staff, Lettering, 1922; Band, 1921, 1922.

HELEN TAYLOR . . . . . *Denton*

MARY ALICE UNDERWOOD . . *Denton*

Y. W. C. A., Secretary, 1922; Mary Arden Club, 1922; Dramatic Club, 1922.

PAULINE UPTON . . . . . *Poolville*

Y. W. C. A., 1922; Education Exchange, 1922; Current Literature Club, 1922; Parker County Club, Secretary, 1921; Choral Club, 1921.

MATTIE VAIL . . . . . . *Venus*

Y. W. C. A., 1922; Education Exchange, 1922; Mary Arden Club, 1922; Ellis County Club, 1921.

PANSY VARNELL . . . . . *Barry*

Y. W. C. A., Vice-President, 1922; Mary Arden Club, 1922; Physical Education Club, 1921, 1922.

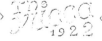

EDITH VERNON . . . . . . *Fate*

Y. W. C. A., 1922; Education Exchange, 1922; Choral Club, 1922.

RUHEY WELCH . *Tapicitoes, New Mex.*

Y. W. C. A., 1922; Current Literature Club, 1922.

TEXANA WILKERSON . . . *Denton*

Y. W. C. A., 1920, 1921, 1922; Education Exchange, 1922; Mary Arden Club, 1921, 1922; Dramatic Club, Vice-President, 1922.

C. S. WILKINSON . . . . . *Denton*

LORINE WILLIAMS . . . *Sweetwater*

Y. W. C. A., 1922; Education Exchange, 1922; Current Literature Club, Secretary, 1921; Vice-President, 1921; West Texas Club, 1921; Choral Club, 1922.

IDA WINKEL . . . . . . *Mason*

Education Exchange, 1922.

RUTH WISDOM . . . . . *Denton*

ULTA E. BROWN . . . . . *Cisco*

Reagan Literary Society, 1922.

Sophomores

RUTH CARTER . . . . *Edgewood*

GOLDIE CULPEPPER . . 1922; *Rowenna*
Education Exchange, 1922; Current
Literature Club, Vice-President, 1922;
Choral Club, 1922.

GRACE FRAZELL . . . . . *Riesel*
Y. W. C. A., 1921, 1922; Mary Arden
Club, 1921, 1922; Dramatic Club, 1922.

VALA FULLINGIM . . . . . *Denton*
Y. W. C. A., Junior Cabinet, 1920,
1921, Reporter Summer Session, 1921,
Senior Cabinet, 1922; Mary Arden, 1922;
Education Exchange, 1922.

ALMA THYRA HATLEY . . *Adamsville*
Y. W. C. A., 1917, 1918, 1921, 1922;
Mary Arden Club, 1922; Lampasas and
Coryell County Club, Secretary and
Treasurer, 1921; Girls' Glee Club, 1922;
Choral Club, 1918.

HATTIE MAYREE JARNAGIN . . *Denton*
Y. W. C. A., 1922; Education Exchange,
1922.

CLARENCE B. JOHNSTON . . *Denton*
Reagan Literary Society, 1922; Press
Club, 1922; Intercollegiate Debater, 1922.

FORREST C. LATTNER . . *Denton*
Reagan Literary Society, 1922; Band,
1922; Baseball, 1922.

Sophomores

JULIA D. McMILLEN . . . *Denton*

T. A. POLLAN . . . . . *Rice*
Lee Literary Society, 1922; Dramatic Club,
1922; Navarro County Club, President, 1921;
Physical Education Club, 1922; Football,
1921; Baseball, 1921.

VIRGINIA POWERS . . . . *Warren*

JULIA SMITH . . . . . *Denton*
Y. W. C. A., Chairman of Music Com-
mittee, 1922; Current Literature Club, 1921;
French Club, 1921; Band, 1921; Choral Club,
Accompanist, 1922; Education Exchange,
1922; Physical Education Club, 1922.

LUCILE WILROY . . . *Huntington*

L. E. WINSTEAD . . . . *Jermyn*
Education Exchange, 1922.

LILLIAN RANEY . . . . *Denton*
Y. W. C. A., 1922.

Sophomores

HERMIA BURGOON . . . . *Denton*

MRS. MINNIE BURTIS CHATHAM, *Frankston*

MRS. FLORENCE CORKERN . *Denton*

MARY DANIEL . . . . *Quitman*

ARLIE DIAL . . . . *Childress*

EDITH EMBRY . . . *McGregor* .

MYRTLE FOWLER . . . *Mansfield*

LEONA HORN . . . . *Prosper*

MAUD MUELLER . . . . *Lipan*

IRENE MURPHY . . . . *Kilgore*

MAURINE RAY . . . . *Tyler*

JOHN A. ROBERTS . . . *Avoca*

ELVIE MAE SALING . . *Celina*

NELL TRAMMELL . . *Fort Worth*

JOSEPHINE WAINSCOTT . . . *Hamlin*

VERA WALKER . . . . *Denton*

FRESHMAN

Freshmen

BLANCHE ADAMS............*Denton*	MURREL BONER.............*Denton*
T. W. ADKINS..............*LaFayette*	NELLIE BOUNDS............*Weatherford*
A. A. ALLEN................*Wills Point*	LUCILE BOSWELL............*Bishop*
MABLE ALLEN...............*Rice*	ANNIE LEE BOYD...........*Midlothian*
LUCY MAE AUGUSTINE........*Ozona*	PAULINE BOYD..............*Mart*
WELTA ANGEL...............*Plano*	NORRIS BROWN.............*Leonard*
PEARL BADGER..............*Decatur*	ONAS L. BROWN............*Edgewood*
VIRGIE BLACKWELL..........*Chireno*	ANDRE BROWN..............*Olney*
MILDRED BLAND............*Ennis*	ABBEY BROWN..............*Friendswood*
MARY BONER...............*Denton*	MILDRED CANTRELL.........*Whiteright*

Freshmen

RUTH CARDEN..............*Denton*	MILDRED DEVENPORT.........*Pilot Point*
EFFIE MAE CASH...........*Weatherford*	MILDRED DOUGLASS.........*Denton*
WILLIE CHRISTIAN.........*Kerens*	NINA DOUGLAS..............*Quitman*
SUE M. CLAY..............*Tyler*	ZOE BELLE EATON..........*Trinidad*
CECIL COOPER.............*Denton*	DONA EDGEMAN..............*Mansfield*
LIDA COOPER..............*Denton*	D. A. EDWARDS.............*Ireland*
CORINNE CURRY............*Mart*	IMA E. ELLIOTT............*Avery*
CARL DARNELL.............*Grand Saline*	NANCY ELWOOD..............*Marshall*
LEVA DAVIS................*Olney*	RUTH EVANS................*Nevada*
EVELYN DAWSON............*Canton*	OLIVIA FERGUSON...:........*Leonard*

Freshmen

Vernice Foster............*Venus*	W. M. Hatley.............*Adamsville*
Blanche Garber...........*Ranger*	Sadie Hamlin.............*Waxahachie*
Irene Gaston.............*Lewisville*	Eula Mae Hester..........*Denton*
Corine Gibson............*Melissa*	Joe Hickman.............*Leonard*
Pauline Goode............*Denton*	Wyona Hill...............*Morgan*
Eva Grady................*Denton*	E. B. Holley.............*Adamsville*
Lenie Gray...............*Vera*	Nora Hughes.............*Center*
Fannie Bell Thaggard......*Queen City*	Olive Jackson............*Elgin*
Norma Harnesberger.......*Dallas*	Harold Jenkins............*Quanah*
Vera Hart................*Smithland*	Aetna Jones..............*Camp Springs*

Freshmen

BEVERLY JONES............*Rockwall*	MAMIE MAXWELL.........*Kirkland*
VALDA JONES..............*Valley Mills*	NANCY McANALLY........*Megargel*
HAZEL KIRKPATRICK......*Denton*	ADDIE McCONNICO........*Kerens*
EDITH KLINGLESMITH......*Denton*	JAMES A. McDONALD......*Hester*
ULYS G. KNIGHT..........*Ponder*	THELMA McKINNEY........*Denton*
BESSIE MAE KUHN........*Denton*	MAY McGLOTHLIN.........*Lamkin*
H. H. LONDON............*Bailey*	VERNA McGLOTHLIN.......*Lamkin*
RUTH LYNN...............*Denton*	GRACE MILLER............*Denton*
GLADYS MARTIN.. ....*Denton*	ALYNE MILLER............*Sanger*
HELEN MARTIN...........*Denton*	FLORINE MILLS...........*Sulphur Springs*

Freshmen

Mary Money..............*Denton*	Neal Porter..............*Belton*
Ray Morris..............*Lindale*	Ruby Roark..............*Leonard*
Mrs. Elizabeth Morris.....*Fort Worth*	H. E. Roberts............*Denton*
Eleanor Myers...........*Marshall*	Henry Robertson..........*Era*
Gladys Peeler.............*Dallas*	Karin Rowan.............*Whitney*
H. A. Perryman...........*Denton*	Ethel Russel.............*Haskell*
Ina Pierce...............*Denton*	Parker Shofer............*Valley Mills*
Edward Pierce...........*Wellington*	Roberta Copeland.........*McKinney*
W. D. Pollan.............*Rice*	Katherine Scharlock......*Bishop*
Lota Price...............*Montalba*	Alta Sherrill.............*Midlothian*

Freshmen

FRANCES SIMMS.........*Personville*	LA UNA SWAFFORD.......*Rice*
MARY E. STAPLES.........*Ponder*	ELLEN TACKER..........*Vernon*
LILLIAN SHIPP...,.......*Addington, Okla.*	FRANK TAYLOR..........*Waxahachie*
LOUISE SMITH............*Vernon*	BONNIE TAYLOR.........*Melissa*
VERA SPEARMAN.........*Venus*	FLORENCE TERRY........*Denton*
EFFIE SPRINGFIELD.......*Springtown*	RUTH THOMASON..........*Memphis*
PAULINE SUDDUTH.......*Welview*	JESSIE TUCKER...........*Clarksville*
LENA STROTHER..........*McKinney*	FLORENCE VANDIVIER .....*Decatur*
MARVIN M. SWEATMAN....*Tolbert*	RENA MAE WAGGONER....*Denton*
KATE SWAFFORD..........*Ponder*	GLADISE D. WAINSCOTT....*Hamlin*

1922

Freshmen

LA MARYLIS WALL..........*Poolville*	OTIS BENHAM...............*Crowell*
RENA WALKER.............*Denton*	CLARA BROWN..............*Leonard*
NAOMI WALSCHAK..........*Buckholts*	ALLIE MAY CLEMENTS.......*Copperas Cove*
THYRA A. WATSON..........*Barry*	OREL F. COLEMAN.....'.....*Whitney*
ZELMA WHITE.............*Frisco*	JOHN DAVIS.................*Denton*
ESTHA WILLIAMS............*Reagan*	THOMAS DAVIS ....*Denton*
CLINT WILKES.............*Denton*	WINNIE DEARING...........*Grapevine*
WM. F. WILKINSON.........*Lewsiville*	WILLIS FLOYD..............*Whitesboro*
LYDA WILKINSON..........*Harrold*	HAZEL HAYES..............*Crowell*
EDNA WOOD..............'....*Olney*	LUCILLE HEMPHILL..........*Italy*

Freshmen

VIOLET JACOBS.............*Valley Mills*	VELMA POOL.................*Troup*
MARY JONES................*Belton*	SAM W. RANEY.............*Alvord*
PHILIP KING................*Atlanta*	E. N. ROSS.................*Denton*
R. W. McCLESKY...........*Dalhart*	FERN STEPHENS............*Weatherford*
IVAN P. OLIVER.............*Denton*	CARROLL WILSON...........*Edgewood*
VIRGIE POLSER............*Hebron*	ELIZABETH WRIGHT.........*Denton*

BERTIE YEARBY.............*Ennis*

Mary, Don't You Weep

I don't know why old Simmons wants to come here fir,
This Old Normal ain't no friend to her,
'Cause she went an' got drown--ed,
Oh, Normal, don't you weep.

(Chorus)
Oh, Normal, don't you weep, don't you mourn,
Oh, Normal, don't you weep, don't you mourn,
'Cause Old Simmons got drown--ed,
Oh, Normal, don't you weep.

Weep like a willow and mourn like a jane,
You can't get to Heaven 'less you win this game,
Old Simmons got drown--ed,
Oh, Normal, don't you weep.

(Chorus)

SECOND YEAR

Second Year

BYRON ALSTOT............*Crandell*
PEARL AUSTIN............*Denton*
EDITH BALL..............*Lillian*
MARY BEGEMAN...........*Electra*
AMMA BORDERS...........*Newark*
DOLLIE BOWEN...........*Flooming Grove*
BILLIE BURTIS............*Frankston*
LOUISE BUTLER...........*Oak Grove, Ky.*
THELMA BUTTRELL........*Denton*
BLANCHE BRYANT.........*Frost*

GEORGIA LEE CARRADINE..*Delia*
JEWELL CATO............*Thalia*
MINNIE CHAMBERS........*Adamsville*
PAULINE CLARK..........*Cumby*
JAS. O. COFFEY...........*Aubrey*
F. A. COFFEY.............*Aubrey*
THURMAN COLLIER........*Ponder*
GLADYS COLVIN...........*Flint*
THEO. DAVIS.............*Boyd*
JEWELL DOBBS...........*Rice*

Second Year

Eunice Dodd..............*Crowell*	Cleo Gilliam ....*Ambrose*
Allene M. Derryberry.....*Admiral*	Lillie Gillespie...........*Scurry*
Clara Dyer................*Rice*	Mrs. Myrtle Lula Hatley..*Adamsville*
Ima Elliott................*Moran*	Leland Hardegree.........*Ben Wheeler*
Allene English............*Frost*	Mackie Henslee...........*Caldwell*
Mary Ferguson............*Duncanville*	Fannie Lou Hogan.........*Chisholm*
Opal Freeman..............*Moran*	John M. Hooper...........*Denton*
Mattie D. Goforth........*Overton*	Helen Hopkins............*Duncanville*
Grace Garner..............*Dawson*	Lula Hyatt................*Carbon*
Jewell Gilliam ....*Ambrose*	Leda Jackson..............*Ponder*

Second Year

BERTHA JOHNSON............*Iowa Park*	AUDRY MALONE............*Springtown*
CLAUDE JONES..............*Orth*	IRA CECIL MANIRE..........*Ryan*
AUBRA JONES...............*Mullin*	C. R. MATTHEWS...........*Thalia*
RUTH KENNY................*Fort Worth*	KATHERINE MAXWELL.......*Greenwood*
HELEN KEPLINGER...........*Italy*	H. D. MAXWELL............*Lometa*
JESSIE LANGLEY............*Thalia*	MADELENE MAXWELL.......*Blum*
IMOGENE LIEB..............*Albany*	INEZ MCCARLEY............*Tenaha*
RUTH LILLEY...............*Whitehouse*	FAY MCGLOTHIN.............*Lamkin*
H. B. LONDON..............*Bailey*	ZYLLA M. MEISENHEIMER....*Lillian*
LAWRENCE MAYO...........*Jermyn*	MARGARET MENAFEE........*Tenaha*

Second Year

Ione Mitchell..............*Corsicana*	W. B. Patterson...........*Kerens*
Mrs. Lena Morrow........*Winnsboro*	Raymond Patterson........*Adamsville*
W. O. Morrow.............*Winnsboro*	C. C. Perryman...........*Forestburg*
Effie Morris..............*Lewisville*	A. P. Pitt.................*Lindale*
Ida Muncy.................*Krum*	Alice Riggs...............*Tioga*
Nennie Nash..............*Springtown*	Lena Roberts.............*Avoca*
Ora Neill.................*Gorman*	Mattie Mae Seaborn......*Ponder*
Fred O'Dell................*Edna*	Opal Shipley..............*Crandall*
W. H. Oliver..............*Canton*	S. H. Shipley.............*Crandall*
Esther O'Shields..........*Denton*	Eolin Esther Simpson......*Fort Worth*

Second Year

Mary Sloan..............*Dublin*	Grace Swafford...........*Ponder*
Perry Smith..............*Alvord*	Mabel Swafford...........*Rice*
Verne T. Smith...........*Denton*	Willie Mae Swafford......*Ponder*
Annie Bess Stephens.......*Eden*	Effie Mae Taylor.........*Eden*
Iris G. Stevenson.........*Denton*	Perry V. Travis..........*Valley Mills*
Irene Stout..............*Denton*	Lora Wainscott...........*Hamlin*
Ida Stuart...............*Denton*	Mae Wornell.............*Blum*
Mack Stuart.............*Denton*	Minerva Webb............*Krum*
Fanny Squires............*Everman*	Bessye Whiteley.........*Florence*
Evelyn Summy............*Mullin*	Laura Wilhelm...........*Vernon*

Second Year

ALBERTA WOOD..............*Argyle*   LELLA WOODRUFF...........*Gunter*
MAE VESTAL...............*Eastland*

The Normal team is out today
To win the game and walk away,
We're "gonna" win this game today
It makes no difference what they say.

We know you will
We know you can
You're the best old team in all the lan';
Come on boys—Don't mind the heat,
Stay in there—We "gotta" beat.

Wild and woolly—Wild and woolly,
Bust a Broncho—Beat a Bully,
Hootin'—Tootin'—Cuttin'—Shootin'
We're the gang that does the rootin'.

They say that ol' Normal she ain't got no pep
She's pep every step—Pep every step;
They say that ol' Normal she ain't got no pep
She's pep every step, every step.

They say that ol' Normal she ain't got no style
She's style all the while—Style all the while;
They say that ol' Normal she ain't got no style
She's style all the while, all the while.

Fight for the Normal
Normal must win,
Fight to the finish
Never give in;
Rah—Rah—Rah—
You do your best, boys,
We'll do the rest, boys,
Fight for the victory.

First Year

RUTH COX . . . . *Midlothian*
TRESIE DEATON . . . . *Fate*
NELLIE FRANCIS . . . . *Celina*
WILMA AILEEN HAMLETT . . . . . *Denton*
MARIE HAMLETT . . . . *Denton*
E. C. HATTON . . . . *Center*
LOTTIE KINCANNON . . . . *Bruceville*
W. C. MATHIS . . . . *Pritchett*

JOE MCGAUGHEY . . . . *Vera*
FAY MORRISS . . . . *Lewisville*
LILLIAN MORRISS . . . . *Lewisville*
BEN SMITH . . . . *Denton*
C. R. STOCKARD . . . . *Garza*
ISLA TAYLOR . . . . *Bruceville*
CURTIS L. WALKER . . . . *Salesville*
ALFRED WEATHERS . . . . *Snyder*

TRAINING SCHOOL

Training School Seniors

Lora Blair	Willie Geesling
Marion Cameron	Ousley Jones
Annie Laurie Cannon	Roy Klinglesmith
Annie Bell Clements	Robert Lomax
Alice Corbin	Juanita Lowe
Grace Corbin	Griffin Morrel
Flois Crump	Loretta Newton
Floyd Davis	Paul Rogers
Bill Edwards	Pauline Rogers
Dora Floyd	Eugene Wilkins

1922

Eighth Grade

Top Row—BOYD CURTIS, WELDON YERBY, HARWELL SHEPERD, A. S. KEITH, GILBERT GIBBS, CECIL JOHNSON, MYRON STOUT

Second Row—FRANCES NEWTON, GRACE LOVELACE, MARIE MYERS, CASSIE MAE BARROW, BOB E. DRAKE, DELPHINE MILLER, ELLA MARGRÉT CLAYTON

Bottom Row—EVELYN TALLIAFERRO, GEORGIA MAE MARTIN, PAULINE JOHNSON, MARJORIE ROGERS, GEORGIA CORBON, EULALIE WRIGHT, LOUISE BATES

Sixth and Seventh Grades

Top Row—IDERES O'DELL, DORTHY SMITH, INEZ O'DELL, RUTH LOONEY, LOIS UNDERWOOD, EMORY SMITH, JESSIE LEGETT, GEORGE TAYLOR, RICHARD CHRISTAL

Second Row—HELEN WRIGHT, LOTTA EVERS, JEWELL HOOPER, ALICE ADELE WILKIRSON, THELMA CLEMENT, REBECCA DAVIS, BERTIE LEE WYNNE, BEULAH PENDER, ALYNE GOOD

Third Row—MISS HAILE, JOSEPHINE NEWTON, MARGUERITE KLEPPER, JESSIE SIMMONS, VELMA LEE BARTON, JESSIE LONG, HELEN KIMBROUGH, HOMER SMOOT

Bottom Row—CHARLES SMOOT, DOROTHY NELL DOBBINS, RUTH HILL, MATTIE BELLE CUNNINGHAM, GOBER WRIGHT, GEORGE JONES, ERNEST MCCOMBS, JOHN CORBIN, WESLEY UNDERWOOD

Fifth Grade

Top Row—Miss Collier, Irby Grant, Bill Hudspeth, Noble Wright, Ervin Anderson
Second Row—Edra Taliaferro, Frances Wilkins, Wendell Whitehead, Miller Smith, Robert Smith, Elise Vitz, Monia Willcoxon
Bottom Row—Orvamae Swinebroad, Palmer Braly, Allie Standley, Catherine Martin, Ruby Lee Goodger, Gladys Barns

Fourth Grade

Top Row—Miss Myers, Thelma Matthews, Andrew Swenson, Della Louise McCrary, Katherine Schweer, Frances M. Deavenport, Susan Jane Simmons
Second Row—Clark Blackburn, Wilbur Mahan, R. Percy McDonald, Mary Leggett, Jenelle Wynn, Helen Dowell, Berry B. Wright
Bottom Row—Edwyna Craig, Mary Craig, Mary E. Burgoon, Mary Underwood, Elaine Yearby, Willie L. Taylor, Imogene Leggett, Regina.Barnes

Second and Third Grades

Top Row—Mrs. Mizzell, John Vitz, Weldon Underwood, Mary Humphreys, Gladine Fritz, Robert Bradford, Tom Leggett, John Anderson, Joseph Jagoe

Second Row—Robert M. Barnes, Eva Joe Stanley, Mary Jo White, Fred Boon Wright, Herbert Bradford, Herbert Harris, W. C. Dowdell, Sam Underwood, Milton Smith

Third Row—Suzanne Swenson, Walter Miller, Leoland Edwards, Linda Wright, Ina Mae Renfro, Ruby Lee Stockard, Nell Taylor, Silvergray Gray, Annette Henderson, Pearl Wilkins, Willis Miller

Bottom Row—Elizabeth Hoke, Roland Schweer, Hugh Egan, Roberts Grogan, Lottie Mae Donaho, Jessie Deavenport, Bonnie Hudspeth, Isabel Edwards, Christine Shifflett, Eueallie Wright

First Grade

Top Row—Miss Patrick, Howard Floyd, Richard Harris, Alvin Boney, Jim Corbin, Whitney Crow Wright, Grady Beaty, Charles Henderson

Second Row—Charles Saunders, La Vern Klepper, Virginia Craig, Leffel Simmons, Mary Ruth Jarnagan, Ruth Vitz, Mary Jo Wilkins, Selma Rue Blair

Bottom Row—Dorothy Jim Gray, Thomas Matthews, Robert Hopkin, Mary Joyce Talliaferro, Ola Mae Stockard, Milton Martin, Frances Keith Craddock, Pauline Gray, Peggy Hill

Kindergarten

Top Row—Miss Harrimgton, Clydine Oliver, William Botts, Kenneth Armstrong, Davilla Jane St. Clair, Billie Russy, Charles Davis, J. M. Honea

Second Row—Jane Vitz, Mary Joy Odam, Janie Lou Klepper, LeRoy Millican, Hugh Porter, Foster Garrison, Clayton McGinnis

Bottom Row—Jack Brown, Caralee Blackburn, Lily May Hatley, Norman Miller, Jonnie Ruth Leak, George Burgoon, Ralph Smith, L. J. Martin

KINDERGARTEN PARTY

1922

Training School Favorites

ELLA MARGARET CLAYTON

Ella Margaret Clayton is always ready to help with anything and, if she is on a program, she always does her part willingly, and is sure to have it up on time. She is the smaller girls' big sister. She is never too busy to stop and play with them. In class she says very little, but, when she does say something, she says enough to insure her a good grade. This quiet blonde has always had many friends in the Training School, and all of them are glad she is to be with them another year.

ROBERT LOMAX

Robert Lomax has been with us a long time, and we have always known him to be a good sport in the schoolroom, as well as on the playground. Everything is a small matter to Bob; even "Caesar's Campaign" seems to be such a small matter to him that he sometimes overlooks it in his study. He is sure to be your friend with his ever-ready smile and his pleasant word. His auburn hair, which some call red, suggests that he might have a temper, but, if he has, we have never discovered it. We will always remember Bob as a true scout, a fair player, and a dandy pal.

Dedication

MR. J. H. HOPPER

We, the boys of this college who have gone out for the teams, here wish to show our appreciation of Mr. Hopper by dedicating this section to him.

He is about the best friend an athlete has in the college, and his genial disposition and willingness to help have set a splendid example for the men to follow. He seems always to have just the thing we want to borrow, and many's the pipeful of tobacco we have smoked off of him. In the future, when we are out in the world, fighting life's battles, and our minds travel back to our college days and our trials and triumphs on the gridiron, court, or diamond, we shall always think of this great hearted man, whose unquenchable loyalty and undying patience will cause us to look upward and onward in the bigger game of Life.

Appreciation

S. A. BLACKBURN	MRS. A. GRABBE	G. M. CRUTSINGER
Mr. Blackburn is one of the most loyal supporters we have, and it is chiefly through his efforts that the gymnasium has been equipped.	Mrs. Grabbe is the person we always go to after our games to get patched up, and it is through her efforts that the football men were able to keep going.	Mr. Crutsinger, because of his unselfish work for athletics in this college, deserves a place in the heart of every athlete. He is our representative in the T. I. A. A. and is Chairman of the girls' T. I. A. A.

CHARLES LANGFORD

Charles was our yell leader, and his matchless leadership was largely responsible for the support given to the basket ball team by the student body. This support was a great factor in our championship chase.

Wearers of the

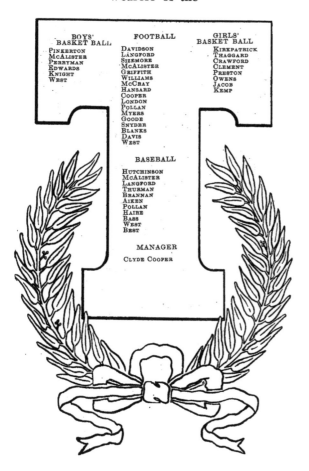

BOYS' BASKET BALL

PINKERTON
MCALISTER
PERRYMAN
EDWARDS
KNIGHT
WEST

FOOTBALL

DAVIDSON
LANGFORD
SIZEMORE
MCALISTER
GRIFFITH
WILLIAMS
MCCRAY
HANSARD
COOPER
LONDON
POLLAN
MYERS
GOODE
SNYDER
BLANKS
DAVIS
WEST

GIRLS' BASKET BALL

KIRKPATRICK
THAGGARD
CRAWFORD
CLEMENT
PRESTON
OWENS
JACOB
KEMP

BASEBALL

HUTCHINSON
MCALISTER
LANGFORD
THURMAN
BRANNAN
AIKEN
POLLAN
HAIRE
BASS
WEST
BEST

MANAGER

CLYDE COOPER

The Coaches

J. W. St. Clair

Mr. St. Clair has charge of the basket ball and baseball teams here. He thought he could quit coaching and be satisfied with the joys of a business life, but the call was too strong and he came back. He signalized his return by putting out a championship basket ball team. He is "a man's man."

T. J. Fouts

Mr. Fouts has charge of football and track, and, in addition to being a good coach, he is one of the best friends an athlete in this school has. Having a keen insight into human nature, he knows just how to get along with the men and get out of them the most that is in them.

The 1921 Football Squad

*Top row—*Sizemore, Goode, Cooper, West, Myers, Langford, McAlister, Davidson, Davis, Griffith.
*Second row—*G. M. Crutsinger, Clyde Cooper, Murray, Williams, Snyder, Hooper, Jack London, Bentley, McCray, Coach Fouts.
*Third row—*Humphries, London, January, Noah, Brewster, Fox, Vickers, Smith, D. Hansard.
*Bottom row—*Jones, Lorrance, Winstead, Perryman, McClure, Brawley, Blanks.

Season's Games

Normal	41	Grubbs	6
Normal	0	Simmons	6
Normal	0	John Tarleton	13
Normal	33	Wesley	7
Normal	61	Burleson	12
Normal	0	San Marcos	14
Totals	135		58

Review of Football

WHEN the roll was called to fall out for training camp this year, it was found that Coach Fouts had Capt. Goode, Langford, Meyers, Cooper, Davidson, Hansard, McCray and McAlister of last year's eleven to build the team around, and with these eight men and several class stars and high school men, the work of moulding a winning team was soon under way.

The training camp was located at Taylor's Lake, north of Denton, and as soon as the team arrived, their schedule of training was mapped out. The routine was something like this: swimming, breakfast, an hour of rest, two hours' practice, swimming, dinner, rest, another workout, swimming, supper, and then such innocent pastimes as dominoes and "42." At nine o'clock each one would get his blankets, repair to some secluded nook, and sleep the sleep of utter exhaustion.

In reviewing the season, one must take into consideration the wonderful fighting spirit showed by the team, as well as the games won and lost and the scores. The team was outweighed and sometimes outplayed, but never outfought. At San Marcos, although outweighed and almost suffocated by the depressing heat, the team won the admiration of every one present by their undying gameness and their fight.

We lost three games and won three, for a total of 135 points to our opponents 57, which is no mean record, if one takes into consideration the class of teams we were playing and the records they made over the state.

All of this year's team, with the exception of four old veterans, Cooper, Myers, Goode and McAlister will be back next year, and the Normal will be sure to be represented by a snappy bunch. Here's wishing them luck!

It is rumored that there will be a two weeks' training camp next year; if so, the team should be in great trim for the Bears.

The Games

NORMAL   41   The Normal team opened its season in Denton this year,
GRUBBS   6   playing the Grubbs Vocational College team from Arlington.
                  This game was never in doubt, as the Normal team out-
classed the visitors in all departments of the game from whistle to whistle. And
after Meyer's brilliant run in the first few minutes of play, the touchdowns piled
up with a monotonous regularity. Meyers probably played the best game for
Denton, both on offense and on defense, but the whole team was playing unbeatable ball that day.

NORMAL   0   The Cowboys brought an "honest-to-goodness" football team
SIMMONS   6   here to play the Normal, and the spectators were furnished a
                  real battle to watch. The Normal was playing against over-
whelming weight, but even then put up one of the prettiest exhibitions of game
defensive playing that was ever seen on our grid, and it was only after almost
superhuman efforts that the Cowboys were able to put over their lone touchdown. Moreover, the Normal should not feel bad over this defeat, as Simmons
defeated Trinity, T. C. U., and other big teams in the T. I. A. A. by larger scores
than that by which they defeated us.

NORMAL   0   John Tarleton caught us on an off day, a day when
JOHN TARLETON 13   we should have played real football and avenged
                  the defeat of last year but failed to do so. The
Normal team could not work together, and our defense was rather poor, compared
with that of previous games, especially on breaking up defense passes. However due credit should be given to John Tarleton, who did show a pretty good
brand of ball. Especially was Aikens, their big fullback, worthy note. He was
a good punter and his receiving of passes went far toward the Normal's undoing.
Let us hope for better results next year.

NORMAL   33   The team next played away from home, going to Greenville
WESLEY   6   to meet the Wesley College Panthers. The Normal was
                  right that day, and quoting from the Greenville Herald,
"The shades of night fell on a tragedy that read, Normal 33, Wesley 6." The
team ran better interference than ever before, and had no trouble in making
long gains around the end and, when a buck was called, the line always responded
nobly. The Wesley team fought bravely but were no match for the speed and
deadly accuracy of the Normal backs and forwards.

NORMAL   61   Normal next met her old enemy, Burleson College, on the
BURLESON 12   local gridiron and administered a severe drubbing to her.
                        The team, as a whole, played well, and by brilliant bursts
of speed was able to run the score up. West stood out above the rest. His
fleetness enabled him to go thru the Burleson defense time and again, and once
on the kickoff he circled the entire Burleson team and ran ninety-yards to a
touchdown. Langford played a good game, both in returning punts, and on
the receiving end of Davidson's long passes.

NORMAL   0   Worn out by a long trip, the Normal was defeated by
SAN MARCOS 14   her fellow teachers at San Marcos. The boys put up a
                           game fight against the overpowering heat and the San
Marcos team, however, and the opponents certainly earned their meager victory.
San Marcos had a good bunch of clean, hard hitting players and, aided by the
afore-mentioned heat, defeated us fair and square, thus taking away from us
the Normal College championship of Texas, which the Denton teams have held
for the past seven years.

BUCK GOODE, *Captain*

Buck played fullback again this year, and there were not very many in the state who could equal him. Although light, he has an uncanny knack of picking holes in the opposing line and few times when he was called upon did he fail to gain the necessary yards. Always cool and alert, he set a splendid example for his men to follow. The Normal will miss this little fullback next year.

GUY DAVIDSON, *Captain-Elect*

Guy started the season at end, but after McCray was injured he was shifted to quarter and played that position for the rest of the season. He is a natural football player; his headwork at quarter pulled us through many a tight place, and his passing was the best seen here in many a day. He was also a good defensive man, playing end on defense. He was unanimously elected to lead the 1922 team.

CHARLES LANGFORD

Charles held down the right wing position again this year, and filled it to the satisfaction of every one who saw him play. He played safety on defense and was good at running back punts, gaining many yards in this way. But he did best on the receiving end of passes. Get a ball anywhere within reach and he had it. The team will lose a good sport in Charles.

BILL MYERS

"Cockeye" played his last game for the Green and White this year, finishing up his fourth season here. He was shifted to halfback the first of the year and filled the place so well that he was kept there the rest of the season. "Cockeye" was a terrific line smasher and could always be depended upon to move his man in the interference.

BILL COOPER

Bill was another of the old veterans, playing his fourth year here. As in former seasons, he played center, and rare was the time that a substitute was needed for him, because Bill just couldn't be knocked out. He was the deadliest tackler we had, and when he hit a man, that man came down. "Who will take the place of William?"

IRVAN WEST

"Irv" was the fastest man on the squad and held down the position of halfback. He was a good defensive man, but his greatest strength lay in his speed in circling the ends. He was the best ground gainer the team had, and was probably high point man on the team. He will be back to help drub our rivals next year.

TED SIZEMORE

This was Ted's first year on the squad, but he showed up so well that he gained a regular berth at left end in the first game. Fast and aggressive, he is the ideal type for a defensive end, and he was especially good at smearing the opposition's end runs. He will be back next year.

WALLACE DAVIS

Davis is a product of Denton High, playing his first year with the Green and White this season. He held down the position of left tackle, and rarely was an opposing team able to gain over his side. Furthermore, he was not an amateur when it came to opening up a hole for the backs to go through.

JACK LONDON

Jack was a product of the class games, but from the very first his aggressiveness and ability to take punishment won him a place at right guard on the regulars, and a lasting place in the hearts of the school. He never knew when to stop fighting. He will be back to administer our opponents some more misery next year.

C. B. SNYDER

Snyder was another man who came in from Denton High this year. He played left guard, and, with his teammate Davis, formed an almost impregnable line. Snyder has several interesting years ahead of him here and will bear watching.

"BITSY" McCRAY

"Ole Man Hard Luck" got after 'Bits'" at the first of the season and got a shade the best of the argument, as "Bits'" got an ankle badly sprained in scrimmage immediately after the Simmons game. Up to this time he was running the team from quarter and playing a jam-up game besides.

JOHN HANSARD

This was John's second year on the squad, and his speed and general all-round ability made him valuable either in the backfield or at end. His best game was against Wesley, where his terrific line plunging gained us many yards and incidentally several touchdowns.

1922.

TIPPIE POLLAN

"Fats" could play any position in the line, and with his great weight he was a hard man to go over. His best game was with San Marcos, where his strength stood him in good stead. His genial disposition made him popular with the men, and everyone is sincerely glad he will be back next year.

BOB BLANKS

Bob, although light, was a good man either at center or at end. He was about the most aggressive player on the entire squad and was one of the surest tacklers. He will be back next year and will probably fill the shoes of Bill Cooper.

I. B. GRIFFITH

"Griff" was the toe artist of the team. His kickoffs reminded one of the days of Fred Cobb and rarely did he miss kicking goal after a touchdown. He was good at end, quarter, and half, and was one of the most versatile men on the squad.

"FRECK" WILLIAMS

"Freck" did not have any football experience when he came out this year, but what he lacked in experience he made up in fight and hard trying. With a little more training he will make a man that will be hard to stop, for he has all the essentials of a player plus the ability to take a lot of punishment.

DAN McALISTER

Dan is an old veteran of the football gridiron, having played for three years on the Normal team. He possesses plenty of grit and fight, but, because of being slightly timid, fears publicity, and would not write up this article, so it was done by one of his assistants. It may be said here that Dan was not on the side lines this year during any game.

CLYDE COOPER
Manager.

TRAINING

CAMP

HOLD THAT LINE

SIMMONS GOES AROUND END

ACTION

WE HIT BURLESON'S LINE

CHARGING

BLOCKING A KICK

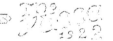

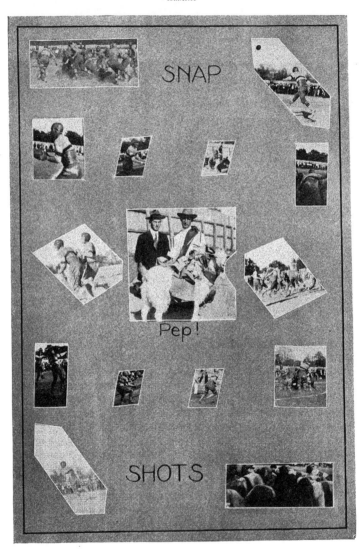

SNAP

Pep!

SHOTS

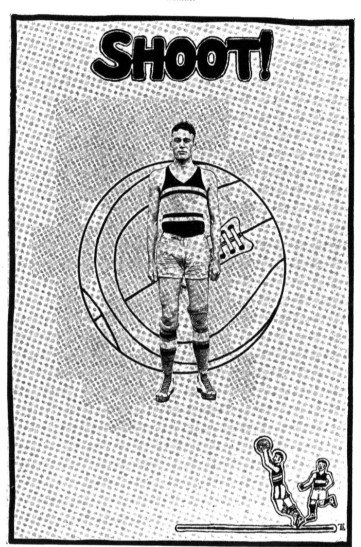

The 1922 Basketball Squad

Top Row—McALISTER, KNIGHT, STEVENS, EDWARDS, PERRYMAN, ST. CLAIR (Coach)
Bottom Row—GRIFFITH, WEST, PINKERTON (Captain), KLEPPER, McCOMBS

The 1922 Season in Basket Ball

WHEN THE referee's whistle blew taps on the 1922 basket ball schedule at Dallas it closed one of the most successful seasons the green and white ever went thru.

When the season opened, Coach St. Clair had two old men back, Captain Pinkerton and McAlister. But there was a wealth of new material, and he began to whip them into shape to meet Southwestern U., who was the first victim of the Normal's championship drive.

Our being admitted to the Texas Intercollegiate Athletic Association gave the men something to fight for and pitted them against some of the strongest combinations in the State. Moreover, it is worthy of note that on our first year out we won a championship from some of the oldest and most established universities in Texas.

We played ten games in the T. I. A. A. conference and won them all. Among those who went down before our onslaught were Southwestern, Austin College, San Marcos, and our traditional rival, Simmons College. Out of the conference we played six games: Two with Tulsa U., one of which we lost by a score of four points, and four at the A. A. U. meet at Dallas, where we went thru to the finals only to lose to the fast Cullem & Boren team. One consolation we can find for this defeat is the fact that Tulsu U. drubbed Cullem & Boren and we beat Tulsa.

There is all probability that all the six men who made letters will be back, and, with this year's practice together, the Normal team next year should make history for the school.

One of the big factors in our victories was the one hundred per cent loyalty of the student body. A team just couldn't help fighting for a bunch such as we had backing us.

The Games

NORMAL vs. SOUTHWESTERN On January fifth we opened our schedule with a game against Southwestern. For the first five minutes it looked as if Southwestern would win, but we finally hit our stride and proceeded to administer a severe defeat to the astonished Pirates to the tune of 47-32.

NORMAL vs. AUSTIN COLLEGE The next week, on January eleventh and twelfth, the Austin College Kangaroos invaded the Eagle lair and got clawed, chawed and mangled to the tune of 31-14 and 39-17. Their five-man defense was very ineffective against the speed of the Eagles' offense.

ROAD TRIP TO SAN MARCOS On January twentieth we embarked on a trip to the homes of the Bobcats and the Pirates, and with the sting of a certain football defeat still rankling in our bosoms, we hopped on the Bobcats and beat them 48-8 and 30-16. One noticeable thing about the games was the fact that several of the opponents' football men were trying to play basket ball.

The next game we played was against the Southwestern Pirates, and this proved to be the crucial game in our race for the championship. Suffice it to say that when the smoke of battle had cleared, it found Herrera and Company on the short end of a 32-29 score, and another name engraved in the hearts of sport followers of the Normal. "Sleepy" Edwards woke up that night and showed the Pirates the art of tossing baskets from all angles and distances of the court. He just couldn't miss.

NORMAL vs. SIMMONS Our next games were at home, where we entertained the Simmons Cowboys. The Cowboys were simply outclassed by the speed and teamwork of the Eagles and had to go back to their wild west satisfied with two defeats, 29-13 and 48-17.

NORMAL vs. TULSA We struck a snag in our next game, when Tulsa beat us 32-28; but the next night we came back and beat them 42-29. These two games were the best played in Denton. Tulsa has a wonderful team, clean and fast; they don't know when to stop playing basket ball.

NORMAL vs. SAN MARCOS San Marcos next came and we continued to show them the fine art of playing basket ball, beating them 50-12 and 46-16.

THE A. A. U.
MEET AT DALLAS
In the A. A. U. meet at Dallas we were pitted against some of the strongest teams in the State, and were finally beaten out in the finals, after playing four games in thirty-six hours. We swamped S. M. U. Freshmen in the opener 50-15, and that night beat the A. & M. Freshmen 30-26. The next day in the semi-finals we beat Trinity Park 32-12; but Cullem & Boren beat us out 29-21 in the finals, and we had to be content with the position of runner-up.

SUMMARY
The Eagles played sixteen games, winning fourteen, for a total of 603 points to the opponents' 317. They were undefeated in the T. I. A. A. Conference and were not defeated by a Texas College or University.

ANYBODY   SLEEPY·
            EDWARDS

"ROSY" PINKERTON

Captain

In Pinkerton the Normal has a center that is without a peer in T. I. A. A. circles. He loves the game and never knows when to stop ringing 'em, for from under the goal or in the center of the court it's about the same to him; and he is a wizard when it comes to dropping them thru from the fifteen foot line.

An all T. I. A. A. selection.

"SLEEPY" EDWARDS

"Sleepy" was our demon forward. Southwestern thought he was seven feet tall, but he is just a little over six feet. He was the star of many of our games, as with his long build and his accurate eye, he was able to ring up many a basket for us. Altho he was not especially fast, he was always at the right place.

He is an all T. I. A. A. forward.

"SNAG" PERRYMAN

"Snag" earned the right to wear his nickname in the Tulsa games, in which he played rings around their fast little Indian forward. He takes the game seriously and is about the hardest working man on the squad. His greatest strength lies in taking the ball off the opponent's backboard. On occasion he can play center with the best of them.

"Galahad" Knight

"Galahad" played opposite Edwards on the other forward, and, with Edwards and Pinkerton, made up one of the best offensive combinations in the State. He was deadly accurate on short shots and could occasionally drop one thru from far out in the field. His genial disposition makes him a favorite with all the men, and we are sincerely glad he will be back next year.

"Puss" West

"Irv" was our fast forward, whose speed helped blaze our victory in the second Southwestern and Tulsa games. He is the fastest man on the squad and could always be depended on to help bring the ball down the court, either on a dribble or by passing. He was good in messing up the opponent's dribble too.

An all around good athlete.

"Stellar" McAlister

Captain-Elect

We can very well call "Mac" the "old reliable," as he played the same steady cool game which has characterized his playing in previous years. It is needless to say that his ability to keep the forwards of opposing teams from scoring had much to do with the winning of the T. I. A. A. championship. We are looking for another championship team in 1923, if Dan comes back.

Athletics at the North Texas State Normal College

THE present academic year has brought a near-crisis in the realm of intercollegiate athletics in the United States, which followed soon after the great furor in organized baseball. It appears that this country was about to lose sight of the main thing in its sports—and to run off after strange gods, or possibly to allow strange gods, or their worshippers, to run off with its sports. This general spectacle has presented nothing new in the way of phenomena connected with human activity. However, it does present a warning of dangers that cannot be overlooked or disregarded by those who are connected with sports in any way; and who have sound ideals regarding their proper place, purpose and development.

The most noticeable athletic commotions during the year have occurred among the well-known eastern colleges and universities, and the larger colleges of the middle west. In these sections, either a new conscience regarding athletics is being evolved or a long dormant one is being revived, as evidenced by the serious study given to the subject by the presidents and other administrative officers of the best known institutions in the land. The standard newspapers and magazines have been and still are carrying studious discussions of the different phases of the general subject of collegiate and scholastic athletics. On the main proposition—that athletics exist for the school and not the school for athletics—there seems to be general agreement. The details of solving the problem toward that end are furnishing the subjects for discussion.

The great American tendency toward commercialism seems to constitute the root of all the evils that are being discussed. Institutions have thought they found in athletic sports a priceless advertising asset, and have appropriated money accordingly, not under a bushel, but rather upon the hilltops of all the headlines they could break into. By some institutions, their cash dividend producing ability has been shown to be a stumbling block in the path to higher things. The alumni and camp followers of various sorts have offered the athletics of their pet institution upon the altar of the great goddess of Chance. Students with some degree of athletic ability, or with none, have seemed to perceive in the sports of the colleges sources of private gain of one sort or another. Young men occasionally exhibit such poor understanding as to write to our Physical Education Department asking: "What can you offer me to come to your school and play?" The time must come when colleges will not even be asked such questions; for it must become an axiom in the land that they cannot betray their ideals for thirty pieces of silver. Clean, wholesome sports exalt a college; but crooked athletics is a reproach to any institution.

During this year, which marked the coming of our College into its seniority, a very considerable amount of study has been given to the question of athletics by the Administration of the College, with a faculty committee on athletics as an active agent. The ideals to be upheld are summarized briefly as follows: First, that the training is the thing and not the score; that a college which must depend on winning games for its advertising has nothing of value to advertise. Second, that time and money spent on sports can be justified only when such expenditure brings the greatest good to the largest number of students. Third, the value and advantages to be derived from athletic contests with other colleges are recognized, as is also the absolute necessity of keeping these intercollegiate relations upon the highest possible plane of sportsmanship.

In working toward these ideals this year, very noteworthy progress has been made at this College. The facilities and equipment for offering the benefits of physical training have been greatly increased. Students have responded by coming out in larger numbers than ever before for training in all branches of sport, and by upholding the same standards of lady-like and gentlemanly conduct on the athletic field as obtains in the classroom. With the very beginning of the year, the rules and regulations of the Texas Intercollegiate Athletic Association were enforced in the boys' sports, because it was believed they represented the best practice in intercollegiate relations. And when this Association met in Dallas on December eighth, the North Texas State Normal College made formal application for membership and was admitted. We have kept the faith as expounded in the book of rules and were fortunate enough to win the Association championship in basket ball. The spirit of wholesome enthusiasm among the student body back of this team, and the conduct and scholarship record of the players have furnished reasons for pride and satisfaction to the entire College. On February twenty-fifth, at the suggestion of our Athletic Committee, the representatives of seven senior colleges of this State met at Texas Woman's College in Ft. Worth and laid definite plans for the formation of the Texas Woman's Athletic Association, which will become operative in controlling the intercollegiate athletic relations of girls' teams with the opening of the next academic year. If intercollegiate athletics survive as a permanent feature of American colleges, it is absolutely necessary that there be open-minded co-operation on the part of all institutions concerned in keeping these activities upon the highest plane of wholesome sportsmanship.

GEO. M. CRUTSINGER,
Chairman, Athletic Committee.

The 1921 Track Squad

Back row—COOPER, GILMORE, W. WEST, FOUTS (Coach)
Front row—HUBBARD, MCALISTER, ROADY, I. WEST, HANSARD

1922 Track Prospects

At the time the Yucca goes to press the prospect for a good track team this season is very pleasing. Several men are working out each day on the cinder path. The track men are somewhat handicapped, however, on account of baseball practice each evening at the same hour and the same place as track practice.

Among the promising material for a winning team are: West, Noah, Knight, McAlister, Pollan, John Hansard, Frank Hansard, Pinkerton, Cooper, Allgood, Langford, and Brown.

In the five-mile cross country run held at Fort Worth on March eighteenth, Frank Hansard ran neck and neck with the famous Young-blood of Texas University and was beaten by him only a few feet, taking second place. Noah took fourth place in this meet.

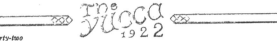

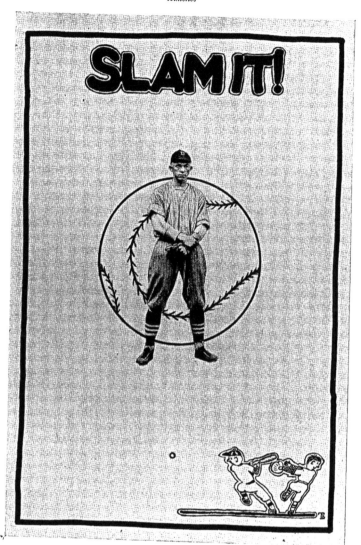

The 1921 Baseball Squad

Back Row—HATLEY, POLLAN, BEST, BASS, McALISTER
Front Row—STARLING, HARE, LANGFORD, AIKEN, WEST, FOUTS (Coach)

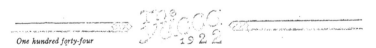

The 1922 Baseball Squad

Top row—JENKINS, BREWSTER, TAYLOR, POLLAN, HANSARD, EDWARDS, SIZEMORE, DAVIS
Front row—MAX WEST, ADAMS, McALISTER, IRVAN WEST, LANGFORD, BALCH

Baseball Prospects for 1922

With four letter men back—West, Langford, Pollan and McAlister—and a large quantity of new material, the baseball prospects for 1922 look bright.

For pitcher Edwards, Goode, Brewster, and Starling are trying out. Bill Cooper seems to have the catcher's place made. For first base, Pollan and Tampke seem to be the most likely candidates. For second base, shortstop and third base, Langford, Knight, West, Taylor, Hansard and Balch are showing up well. Sizemore, Oliver, Davis, and McAlister are the ones likely to fill the outfield positions.

The 1921 Baseball Season

FROM THE standpoint of games won and lost the baseball team of 1921 can not boast very much, but, when one considers that there was only one man on the team who had ever played college baseball before, he can look back on our record with a reasonable degree of pride.

Aikens was the only man of former years to answer to roll call, but, with a wealth of high school men and would-be bush leaguers, coach Fouts went to work and soon had a pretty good combination worked out. However, about this time "ole man hard luck" got on the job, and, by the time of our first game with Decatur, three of our regulars were sitting on the sidelines watching us slaughtered.

Our first game with Decatur was a fiasco. As a result of a high wind, timely hits on the part of our opponents and untimely errors on our part, the smoke the battle cleared from the field with the Normal team holding the short end of a big score.

Our next attempt was much better, as we beat Trinity and their much famed college twirling ace, Edmondson, on their diamond. Bass was pitching invincible ball that day, and with an air-tight defense our team was unbeatable. One fact that should not be overlooked in thinking of this game is that the week after we beat Edmondson he beat A. & M. of Texas by a good score.

Out of last year's team four men—Langford, West, Pollan and McAllister—are back to form a nucleus for this year's nine; so let us look to the future, not to the past.

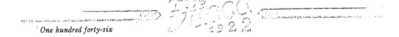

The Games

DECATUR 17
NORMAL 4
The first game we played was with Decatur Baptist College on our own diamond, and, with three regulars on the bench, we did not have a chance. Decatur had a bunch that knew how to hit and a pitcher that knew how to pitch, with the result that they knocked three home runs and a few dozen two-baggers. The one redeeming point that this game afforded was the fact that our outfielders got plenty of track practice.

TRINITY 1
NORMAL 2
This was the game that stood out above the rest of our schedule as the sun's radiance stands out above the star's. It is the bright spot in an otherwise drab season. We were pitted against the mighty Edmondson, who was recognized as one of the best college pitchers in Texas. But we also had a pitcher that day, one who had Edmondson bested in the one thing that makes a pitcher great, coolness under fire. He was Horace Bass. The game was a pitchers' battle from start to finish, and, although we got but one hit, it came at the right time. Trinity's three hits were very well scattered, so well scattered in fact that they were able to cross the plate but once, while our one hit by Aiken and a perfect sacrifice by Pollan pushed two across. Bass, first up for the Normal in the third inning, led off by hitting to third. The third baseman, in his eagerness to make a quick killing, overthrew first, and Bass loped on to second. Aiken came up and hit one down the first base line that went for three bases and Bass counted. Pollan, next up, laid down a perfect bunt and Aiken came home with the run that won the game.

NORMAL 9
DALLAS U 4
The next game we played was at home with out old arch-enemy Dallas University, and on this day we had on our batting clothes, getting thirteen safeties, some of them for extra bases. Bass pitched good ball; most of Dallas U's scores being the result of errors. This was also the game in which Thurman and Langford got back into harness.

DECATUR 5
NORMAL 0
Our next venture was over at Decatur, where a Mr. Kuykendall is the pitcher on their club; and the day he played us he was very much right. He had lots of curves and speed; in short he had everything he needed. And we just could not connect with his offerings.

OTHER GAMES
We played two other games but they were not with college teams. In one, with Argyle, we won 29-5, and in the other, with Denton town team, we won 3-0.

"DOC" AIKENS

"Doc," besides being a good captain, held down the difficult position of shortstop to the satisfaction of every-one who saw him play. Fast and brainy, "Doc" was a good man in the field, at the bat, or on the bases. His place will be hard to fill.

CLAUDE BRANNON

Claude was our regular catcher, and so well did he fill the position that he never had to have a substitute called for him. He was nervy and a hard hitter, and his accurate whip to second cut off many a would-be-steal. His will be another hard place to fill.

THURMAN

Thurman was the hard-luck man on the baseball team, having had an ankle sprained the first few days of practice; but when he did get into the line-up he made up for it by poling them far and near. He could play outfield with the best of them, too.

CHARLES LANGFORD

Charles was our sunfielder, and he filled this position very satisfactorily, receiving many chances that anyone else would have lost in the sun glare and handling them well. He was a fast man on the bases too and will wear a Normal uniform next year.

IRVAN WEST

Although West got a late start, he was soon perched on second base and held that position the rest of the season. Naturally fast, West was both a good infielder and a good man to have on base. He was also about our best sacrifice hitter. He will strengthen the team next year.

EARNEST HUTCHINSON

"Hutch" played his second year at the initial corner, and it is agreed by all critics that he is the best fielding first baseman that ever wore a Normal uniform. He could stretch himself into almost any position in order to get one. He was not a very consistent hitter, but, whenever he did lay against one, it traveled a "fur" piece.

JAKE BEST

"Jake" was the little fellow who held down the hot corner last season and who handled all chances alike. He could whip them across to first from any position, and when he came to bat in a pinch, he always delivered with either a hit or a sacrifice. "Jake's" good humor made him a favorite with his teammates, who will miss him next year.

TIPPIE POLLAN

"Fats has a big bat that resembles Roosevelt's big stick and weighs just as much, and when he advances to the plate the horsehide usually gets a severe pounding. Although he is not a Ty Cobb on the bases, he can hit with the best college hitters and is no slouch in the field.

HORACE BASS

Bass was the mainstay and all the assistants on the pitching staff last season, having pitched every inning the team played. His greatest feat was out-pitching Edmonson of Trinity. Naturally cool and collected, he had everything that a pitcher needs to pitch winning ball. He was a good hitter too.

MARVIN HAIRE

Haire could fill in, either outfield or infield, and was a good man in either place. He had a great throwing arm, could whip them in from deep outfield with great accuracy, and he just couldn't miss a fly ball if it was anywhere in reach.

DAN McALISTER

McAlister was the only three-letter man that the Normal had last year. It seems that he makes a good man wherever he is put. If this does not tell you enough about him, look up any athletic section in the book and you can find some more.

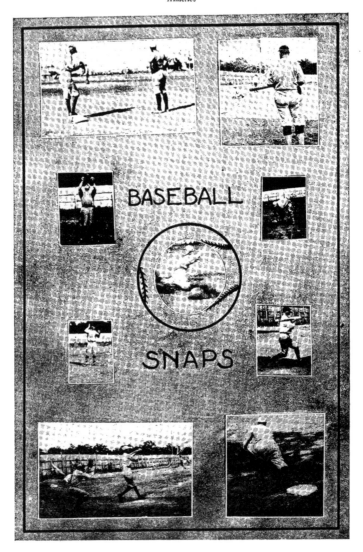

BASEBALL

SNAPS

The Coaches

MISS BEULAH A. HARRISS	MISS VIRGINIA BROADFOOT

It is useless to dwell on the successes that Miss Harriss has made in the way of moulding basketball teams. She is one of the best coaches in the Southwest for a girls' basketball team. A few times during the past season the score at the end of the game has been against her team, but one of the great principles she has taught her players is to know how to take defeat as well as victory.

Miss Broadfoot is one of the best friends a student could have. As a director of Physical Education she has very few equals. You will not be able to find a person in the Normal who is more willing to get behind a college activity and help to put it over than is Miss Broadfoot.

The 1922 Girls' Basketball Squad

Top row—CLEMENT, KEMP, HARRISS (Coach), JACOB, CRAWFORD
Front row—LILLIAN PRESTON, LOUISE PRESTON, OWENS, THAGGARD, KIRKPATRICK

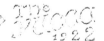

The 1922 Season in Girls' Basket Ball

WHEN basket ball practice began for this season it was found that only two members of last year's squad had returned to the Normal this year. Using these two players as a nucleus, Miss Harriss went to work to build up a winning team. Of course, it was a very difficult task to replace the famous Thorne twins and Cecil Owens, who starred on the team last year. After a few workouts, however, Rubylea Clement and Queen Thaggard were placed in the forwards' positions and filled them satisfactorily through the entire season, and Ina Owens, a sister of Cecil and Captain of this year's squad, was the best prospect for center. She, too, must be given credit for playing a good game all season. Katherine Kemp, a veteran of 1921, Ruby Crawford, Nell Kirkpatrick, Violet Jacob and Louise Preston showed up well also.

The team this year was defeated a few times but by very close scores. This by no means signifies that the season was a failure; it was far from that.

Let us all turn to the future—to the prospects of a championship team in 1923, which are very bright indeed. The girls are in the T. I. A. A. now. Let's bring the trophy for the girls' T. I. A. A. to Denton next year.

The Record

Normal	18	John Tarleton	19
Normal	24	Commerce	20
Normal	9	S. M. U.	18
Normal	22	San Marcos	15
Normal	39	Wesley	11
Normal	20	T. W. C.	28
Normal	34	San Marcos	37
Normal	16	Southwestern	12
Normal	25	Commerce	29
Normal	14	Southwestern	12
Total	221	Total	201

The Games

NORMAL 18
JOHN TARLTON 19
The season was opened on the home court with John Tarlton. The unusual weight and height of the opponents showed no great results against the rapid team work of the local players. Two minutes before the final whistle the score was tied, but a foul on the Normal made the winning point by a free shot for the visitors.

NORMAL 24
COMMERCE 20
The next game brought victory by a hard fight against the old-time rivals of Commerce. The Normal won by two field goals made in the last few minutes of the game. Both teams showed a tendency to be rough, but they were fairly matched for the fight.

NORMAL 9
S. M. U. 18
The first game away from home was played on the S. M. U. court. The Mustanglets took the lead in scoring and maintained it throughout. Even though Denton fought steadily, she never reached her real power. The game was hard, and fouls were too numerous for the maintenance of interest.

NORMAL 22
SAN MARCOS 15
The Normal girls played one of the best games of the year on the home court with the South Texans. Despite the substantial lead San Marcos gained in the first half, Denton came back full force, displaying her real ability in delivering a terrible wallop, which was not present in such quantity in any other game of the entire season.

NORMAL 39
WESLEY 11
Wesley College sextette were our next victims. They fought valiantly, but were forced to retire with heavy losses under the rushing offense of the Normal girls. At no time during the game was the home team uneasy about losing, for each girl was at her best in co-operating with her fellow players.

NORMAL 20
T. W. C. 28
The following Monday the game with T. W. C. was not so fast and fouls were very frequent. Both sides battled in a clean fought game; however, the score was not definitely decided until the final whistle. Excellent teamwork characterized both teams in the first part of the game, but the Normal forwards fell short of consistent field throwing; so they were humbled by the team from Fort Worth in a score of 20-28.

NORMAL 34
SAN MARCOS 37

The team made a big jump next to South Texas for a series of games, but only played San Marcos and Southwestern. They were shown genuine hospitality while in San Marcos. The teams met in good spirits, which resulted in a close fight. The score during the thirty minutes of play was tied five times and at the time of the final whistle stood 34-34. In a five minute play-off San Marcos was just lucky in keeping the ball on her court, making three points. The game, though hard fought, was well refereed, and the Normal girls offer no excuses for their defeat other than the "fate of luck."

NORMAL 16
SOUTHWESTERN 12

By the time the team reached Georgetown, the 'ole'" fighting spirit was running high. Confidence, determination, and a defeat the night before at San Marcos were motives enough for any team to fight for a college back home that was sending "pep" over the wires. Denton never doubted the victory, for her spirit was first rate. The team did not dread returning to Denton with a "lose one —win one" record. It could have been worse.

NORMAL 25
COMMERCE 29

Playing on another's field is a hard lesson in readjustment, which always offers possibility of disaster, especially when rivals meet. Commerce more than doubled the score on the Normal at the close of the first half of a game on the former's court; but it was startling how old Denton came back with gigantic energy and speed in the second half, making a score double that made by Commerce. With a few minutes more the Normal would have shown the East Texans what end of the score they would have left at Commerce.

NORMAL 14
SOUTHWESTERN 10

The return game with the Methodists of Georgetown was easily taken by the Eagle girls on the Normal court. Remarkable qualities as well as quantities of spirit and fight were apparent through the whole game. The score does not indicate the capabilities of either team, for there was practically no scoring. This was the last game the Eagles played. Their final record shows that they won five and lost five.

INA OWENS—*Captain*

"Pop" played the position of jumping center, and, although this was her first year as center for the Normal, she held down the position very satisfactorily. She met several centers that surpassed her in height, but none that could out-jump her. She is a sister of Cecil Owens who played jumping center on the Normal team for four years, and we hope she will be with us as long.

QUEEN THAGGARD—*Business Manager*

As this was Queen's third year as a member of the Normal squad, she was able to hold the position of forward down to a good advantage. A very admirable characteristic is her willingness to sacrifice to her playing mate. She did good work entertaining her guards, especially when the other forward was shooting goals. The spirit with which she always played won the favor of every spectator. We are sorry to say that she is not to be back next year.

VIOLET JACOB

Violet Jacob hails from Valley Mills, having been trained in tactics of basket ball by a former Normal player. She played a fast, yet always a steady, consistent game, which made scoring almost impossible for the opposing team. Her faithfulness and determination in basket ball practice reflected credit upon herself and the Normal. She says she does not like the game; you could not tell it by watching her play.

RUBYLEA CLEMENT

Rubylea was a Denton High product, this being her first year on the Normal team. She played forward and was recognized as the best long shot forward on the field. She played at the line most of the time, and, when the ball came to that end of the court, she was able to secure and retain her grip on it with unusual tenacity.

KATHERINE KEMP

This was Katherine's second year on the Normal squad, and she has developed into a reliable side-center. Her success lay, not in her size, but in her swiftness and in her constant playing of the game. Her "never die" spirit was a great asset to the team. She will not be back next year.

LOUISE PRESTON

Louise is another Denton High product. She rendered wonderful service in the past season as a guard on the Normal team. She was good in blocking goals and was a large factor in keeping down the score of the opposing team. Her optimistic nature won favor with every one. Louise covered every forward against whom she played in the same consistent, satisfactory manner.

RUBY CRAWFORD

Ruby was really a guard, but was able to hold down any of the three positions of guard, side center and forward in a very efficient way. She was a very fast player, and her ability to leave the floor at the most opportune moment lost the ball for the opposing forward time after time. She will be at the Normal again next year.

NELL KIRKPATRICK

Nell deserves special mention for her ability as a side center. She was a fast player and never allowed her opponent to outclass her. She always went into the game to fight and to fight hard. As a mixer, she was perhaps the best on the team. She does not expect to be back next year.

11

The Physical Education Department

Top row—BREWSTER, DAVIS, GOODE
Second row—MCALISTER, PINKERTON, MYERS, COOPER, SIZEMORE, FOUTS
Third row—LANGFORD, BROADFOOT, WELCH, LILLIAN PRESTON, QUEEN THAGGARD, RUTH
    CARTER, WALLACE
Fourth row—LOUISE PRESTON, CLEMENTS, MCGLOTHLIN, MATTIE MAE THAGGARD, STOCKARD,
    OWENS
Front row—ST. CLAIR, HENRIETTA CARTER, LUMLEY, VARNELL, KEMP, BECK, JANUARY, HARRISS

OFFICERS

DAN MCALISTER	*President*
QUEEN THAGGARD	*Vice-President*
INA OWENS	*Secretary-Treasurer*
CHARLES LANGFORD	*Campus Chat Reporter*

The aim of the Physical Education Department is to study the higher principles of physical education, to promote good fellowship among its members, and to encourage the spirit of good sportsmanship and fair play.

Publications

Student Publications Council

Standing—GIBBS, STAFFORD, PATRICK, MASTERS, SWEET, PHILLIPS, DAVIS, WALLACE, STOCKARD
Sitting—PEELER, SMITH, YOUNG, ANDERSON, HUGHES, CURRY, COX

FACULTY SUPERVISORS

W. N. MASTERS	*Finance*
MISS MARIE E. PHILLIPS	*Campus Chat*
MISS MARY C. SWEET	*Yucca*
MISS CORA E. STAFFORD	*Yucca Art*

The work of the Publications Council is to solve the problems which confront the Publications from time to time. The Council selects the Editor and Associate Editors of the Campus Chat and persons to fill vacancies on the Yucca Staff.

Ten faculty members and ten student members make up this Council. The student members are recommended by the faculty committee and appointed by the President of the College.

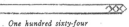

The Yucca Staff

The Campus Chat Staff

Glen Balch
Athletic Editor

Fred C. Hughes
Editor-in-Chief

W. L. Murray
Associate Editor

Ethel Bunch
Dramatic Club Rep.

Ruth Crawford
Kindergartner Rep.

C. A. Davis
A.E.F. Club Rep.

Eugenia Hinderson
C.L.C. Rep.

W. C. Blankenship
Y.M.C.A. Rep.

Vivian Simpson
Choral Club

Ben Roberts
Boys Glee Club

Mattie Mae Thaggard
Girls Glee Club

R. H. Davis
Regan Rep.

Jennie Jenkins
Y.W.C.A. Rep.

C. C. Doak
Silver Strip Rep.

Elizabeth Adams
Mary Arden Rep.

Berla Mae Looney
Associate Editor

Flois Crump
Training School Rep.

LITERARY

Intercollegiate Debating

SOMETIME early in 1907 the boys' literary societies at the Southwest Texas State Normal at San Marcos challenged our Lees and Reagans to a debate. The challenge was accepted, each society electing one speaker. The debate held at Denton was our victory. The challenge was thus informally sent for several years, the victory sometimes settling on the North Texas standard, but more often balancing on the Southwest Texas banner. However, the debates were always conducted on a high·plane of mutual respect and good feeling.

The West Texas Normal College at Canyon wanted to enter the game, and at a meeting of representatives from San Marcos, Canyon, and Denton in Ft. Worth in 1912, the Texas Tri-Normal Debating League was formed, The principal feature of the league plan was that each school should meet each of the other two, all debating the identical question, the home team always having the affirmative. Each school thus supported both sides of the question so that if it were not quite balanced, one school would be exactly as well off as any other. The debates were held on the same night at all three of the schools.

About that time the Department of Reading was organized under the direction of Miss Margaret Price. The Faculty Committee in Intercollegiate Debates was also appointed, of which Miss Blanton, the present State Superintendent of Public Instruction, was an active member. The League raised the debating to a higher level, and Denton was very successful. Of twelve intercollegiate debates in five years, Denton won ten, winning both the affirmative and negative of the question for five years in succession, a record believed to be unique. Two of these debates were with the Durant Normal of Oklahoma, with which school Denton had a special agreement. At present the Texas League is a "pentagonal" affair, each school meeting two other schools one year and the other two the next. It has been suggested that a girls' debating league of the same kind be organized, so that each school would meet each year the boys from two schools and the girls from the other two.

This year Messrs. Floyd and Blankenship go to Commerce. On March 31st Messrs. Johnston and Cronkrite are to match their wits against the debaters from Durant in the Normal auditorium. Messrs. Lemens and Davis are to meet the debaters from the West Texas State Normal of Canyon here on April 21st. The intercollegiate debate exerts its best influence in its reflex effect upon the literary societies. The debate comes only once a year, while the society programs take place every week. No sudden outburst of energy or genius at the time of the intercollegiate debate can outweigh the perennial faithful work of the literary societies. It is only as the latter, with the classes in public speaking, show faithful, earnest effort that any institution can hope to win its share of victories in the intercollegiate debates.

Intercollegiate Debaters

W. W. FLOYD

"He appears to have an unquestioning faith that truth will prevail when presented."

Floyd is a student and a man; of sober mein but jolly soul. His will, bent on success, we predict, will lead him whither we know not. He is a member of the Lee Literary Society, and of the Dramatic and the Choral Clubs.

W. C. BLANKENSHIP

"Great men are they who see that spiritual is stronger than any material force, that thoughts rule the world."

Blankenship has the honor of twice representing his college in debate. We remember his success of 1921. He is an earnest Y. M. C. A. worker, a Regan and chairman of the Student Faculty Council.

Question—Resolved: That a law should be enacted embodying the principles of the Towner-Stirling Bill, creating a Department of Education, and appropriating Federal funds for educational purposes.

Affirmative . . . East Texas State Normal College

Negative . . . North Texas State Normal College

Debated at Commerce, April 21, 1922

Intercollegiate Debaters

THOMAS B. DAVIS, JR.

"Truth is the summit of being; justice is the application of it to affairs."

Thomas is a youthful aspirant in the field of oratory. He is a sturdy chap of high ideals, on which he is building a foundation for the realization of his aspirations.

He is a faithful member of the Y. M. C. A. and of the Lee Literary Society.

W. V. LEMENS

"He that is commanded by truth is self-commanded."

Lemens is a genial man and a willing worker. We expect his earnestness of purpose to lead to the successful attainment of his ideals.

He is prominent in the Y. M. C. A. work and the Lee Literary Society.

Question—Resolved: That a law should be enacted embodying the principles of the Towner-Stirling Bill, creating a Department of Education and appropriating Federal funds for educational purposes.

Affirmative . . . North Texas State Normal College

Negative . . . West Texas State Normal College

Debated at Denton April 21, 1922.

Intercollegiate Debaters

CLARENCE B. JOHNSTON

"Half his strength he puts not forth."

When he begins to speak, we immediately sense defeat for his opponents. His penetrating eye, his keen perception of the inadequacy of the opposition, react in greater self-confidence, and, once begun, the battle is half won!

He is a member of the Reagan Literary Society.

J. B. CRONKRITE

"He conquers because his arrival alters the face of affairs."

We occasionally find a man who is able to hold down a household and a public platform at the same time! This distinction falls to Cronkrite. His fund of good nature and his natural persuasive ability are factors contributing to his ability.

He is a member of the Reagan Literary Society.

Question—Resolved: That a law should be enacted embodying the principles of the Towner-Stirling Bill, creating a Department of Education, and appropriating Federal funds for educational purposes.

Affirmative . . . . Durant State Normal College

Negative . . . . North Texas State Normal College

Debated at Denton March 31, 1922, and won by the N. T. S. N. C. team.

John H. Reagan Literary Society

Top Row—STEWART, KEENAN, WINDSOR, DARNELL, PINORTON, WILSON, ADKINS, COFFEY, HINSON, CRONKRITE, SMITH
Second Row—HOLLIS, DOAK, McKIMSEY, MORELAND, SCOTT, ALLEN, FRITZ, MATTHEWS, GRACE, MULLINS, WHITE
Third Row—COLLEY, JOHNSTON, PATRICK, NOAH, ROBERTS, FARREL
Fourth Row—OVERCASH, PRICE, HAYES, McCLOUD, WILKES, KNIGHT, OLIVER, FORD, MATHIS
Fifth Row—WHITE, MOORE, COWAN, JOHNSTON, DAVIS, COWAN, MORROW, BLANKENSHIP
Front Row—JANUARY, DAVIDSON, DUPREE, RAMEY, HARRISON, COLLIER, CHALMERS, DAVIS, PATTERSON, DUPREE

OFFICERS

Fall Term		*Winter Term*	
C. A. DAVIS	*President*	A. V. PRICE	*President*
RALPH PATRICK	*Vice-President*	C. W. OVERCASH	*Vice-President*
A. A. ALLEN	*Secy.-Treas.*	C. L. MULLINS	*Secy.-Treas.*
W. C. BLANKENSHIP	*Critic*	FRANK JOHNSTON	*Critic*
L. L. FRITZ	*Sgt.-at-Arms*	ULYS KNIGHT	*Sgt.-at-Arms*
C. C. DOAK	*Chaplain*	ARTHUR JONES	*Chaplain*
R. H. DAVIS	*Campus Chat Reporter*		

Spring Term

L. L. FRITZ . . . . *President*
FRANK JOHNSTON . . . . *Vice-President*
E. M. PRYOR . . . . . *Secy.-Treasurer*
C. W. OVERCASH . . . . . *Critic*
R. L. NEAL . . . . . *Sgt.-at-Arms*
A. M. WILSON . . . . . *Chaplain*

The Reagan Representatives

L. L. FRITZ   A. V. PRICE

Question—Resolved, That the suspended sentence in the State of Texas should be abolished.
Affirmative—Reagan Literary Society.
Negative—Lee Literary Society.

The Lee Representatives

F. C. HUGHES   W. L. MURRAY

Robert E. Lee Literary Society

Top Row—WEST, MCALISTER, B. COOPER, BROWN, BRYAN, DAVIS
Second Row—DAVIS, MURRAY, LONDON, McDONALD, WILSON, MAXEY, J. H. McGAUGHEY
Third Row—LANGFORD, SIZEMORE, CALDWELL, FLOYD, STEPHENS, PATTERSON, ADAMS
Fourth Row—COOPER, CORRY, YOUNG, ODELL, ANDERSON, CONNELL, SMITH
Fifth Row—MARTIN, JOE McGAUGHEY, ROADY, LEMENS, EDWARDS, M. D. McGAUGHEY, BALCH
  GALE
Front Row—NEELY, HUGHES, HAYES, BREWSTER, ONAS BROWN, W. F. BROWN, HATTEN

OFFICERS

Fall Term		*Winter Term*	
FRED C. HUGHES . . *President*		C. J. NEELY . . . *President*	
J. A. McDONALD . *Vice-President*		C. L. CALDWELL . *Vice-President*	
THOMAS DAVIS : . *Secretary*		GLEN O. BALCH . . *Secretary*	
VERNON LEMENS . . *Treasurer*		E. M. CONNELL . . . *Critic*	
C. L. CALDWELL . . *Critic*		JACK LONDON . . *Sgt.-at-Arms*	
TIPPIE POLLAN . *Sgt.-at-Arms*		J. A. McDONALD . *Chaplain*	
M. D. McGAUGHEY . . *Chaplain*		D. A. EDWARDS } . . *Tellers*	
JACK GALE } . . . *Tellers*		J. N. BROWN }	
PHILIP KING }			

Spring Term

E. M. CONNELL . . . . . *President*
H. H. LONDON . . . . . *Vice-President*
WILLIS FLOYD . . . . . *Secretary*
J. A. McDONALD . . . . . *Critic*
DEAN DAVIS . . . . . *Sgt.-at-Arms*
W. F. BROWN . . . . . *Chaplain*
W. H. SIMS } . . . . *Tellers*
TED SIZEMORE }

Current Literature Club

OFFICERS

MISS WILSON			SOPHIA BAUER	
MISS MORLEY	} *Club Leaders*		MYRTLE GRIMES	} *Delegates to*
MRS. JOHNSON			LOUISE SMITH	*City Federation*

First Term

LILLIAN MASSINGILL	.	.	*President*
LORINE WILLIAMS	.	.	*Vice-President*
MATTIE SMITH .	.	.	*Secretary*
JIMMIE JENKINS .	.	.	*Treasurer*
MYRTLE GRIMES {			
ETHEL HEATH {	.	*Sergeants-at-Arms*	

Second Term

OTA BELLE MCCAIN	.	.	*President*
LETA BAYLESS	.	.	*Vice-President*
PEARL JANUARY	.	.	*Secretary*
GRACE CALDWELL	.	.	*Treasurer*
WYONA HILL }			
MAUDE CRAVEN }	.	*Sergeants-at-Arms*	

Third Term

ESSIE BALL .	.	.	*President*
GOLDIE CULPEPPER	.	.	*Vice-President*
LOUISE SMITH .	.	.	*Secretary*
CONWAY CRIDER .	.	.	*Treasurer*
MRS. PARKER }			
PEARL RAGLE }	.	*Sergeants-at-Arms*	

ROLL OF MEMBERS

ESSIE BALL	CORINNE CURRY	PEARL JANUARY	LILLIAN SLOAN
LETA BAYLESS	MINNIE DEARING	JIMMIE JENKINS	RUTH SMITH
SOPHIA BAUER	NINA DOUGLAS	LILLIAN MASSINGILL	LOUISE SMITH
GRACE BECK	MILDRED DAVENPORT	LEE MCCLOTHLIN	MATTIE SMITH
AMMA BORDERS	LILLIAN ELDER	MAY MCCLOTHLIN	NELLIE SMYRE
GRACE CALDWELL	LILLIAN FILGO	MINA MCLENDON	JULIA STAFFORD
MAUDE CRAVEN	MYRTLE GRIMES	EFFIE MCLEOD	GENE TAYLOR
CONWAY CRIDER	RUTH GRAY	MAMMIE MAXWELL	JESSIE TUCKER
RUTH CARTER	GLADYS HARISTON	OTA BELLE MCCAIN	LYDA WILKINSON
GOLDIE CULPEPPER	EUGENIA HENDERSON	MRS. BERTHA PARKER	RUHEY WELCH
ETHEL COOPER	WYONA HILL	PEARL RAGLE	LORINE WILLIAMS
NORA COOK .	ETHEL HEATH	IZETTA SPARKS	PAULINE UPTON

Mary Arden Club

Miss Edith Lanier Clark, *Leader*

OFFICERS

First Term		Second Term	
Inez Jones	*President*	Pauline Curry	*President*
Ethel Bunch	*Vice-President*	Bessie Davis	*Vice-President*
Louise Stout	*Secretary*	Grace Frazell	*Secretary*
Ruth Crawford	*Treasurer*	Mary Elizabeth Wright	*Treasurer*
Ina Pierce		Irene Duncan	
Gladys Peeler	*Sergeants-at-Arms*	Alice Riggs	*Sergeants-at-Arms*
Elizabeth Adams	*Chat Representative*	Elizabeth Adams	*Chat Representative*
Emily Hays		Annie Cooper	
Ima E. Elliot	*Delegates to City Federation*	Jessie Lee Cates	*Delegates to City Federation*

ROLL OF MEMBERS

Elizabeth Adams
Ruby Adams
Annie Fay Andrews
Ethel Bunch
Ruth Carden
Mary Carlisle
Jessie Lee Cates
Annie Cooper
Clara Cox
Ruth Crawford
Mary Creswell
Pauline Curry
Bessie Davis
Irene Duncan
Dana Edgeman
Ima E. Elliot
Nancy Ellwood
Helen Emberson

Inez Evans
Grace Frazell
Vala Fullingim
Blanche Garber
Alma Hatley
Emily Hayes
Vivian Huffaker
Nora Hughes
Emma Jasper
Mae Johnston
Ava Johnston
Inez Jones
Katherine Kemp
Berta Mae Looney
Viola Loveless
Odelle Martin
Exa Minter
Eleanor Myers
Va Rue Orndorff

Ina Owens
Ruth Parker
Gladys Peeler
Ina Pierce
Sallie Pierson
Alice Riggs
Karin Rowan
Alma Sims
Louise Stout
Lula Sullivan
Florence Terry
Mattie Mae Thaggard
Mary Alice Underwood
Mattie Vail
Pansy Varnell
Texanna Wilkerson
Ruth Wisdom
Mary Elizabeth Wright

CLUBS

Lillie Bruce Dramatic Club

Top Row—WILKS, ROWAN, FLOYD, JONES.
Second Row—WILKERSON, KNIGHT, HILL, WILSON
Center—MRS. W. H. BRUCE
Third Row—MONEY, BROWN
Fourth Row—POLLAN, CATES, ROADY, EMBERSON, GALE
Bottom Row—CARTER, ROBERTS, ORNDORFF, DAVIS

Lillie Bruce Dramatic Club

Top Row—COMPTON, BALCH, ANGEL, OLIVER
Second Row—FRAZELL, BOYD, PARKER, KIRKPATRICK
Center—MISS CORALEE GARRISON
Third Row—MARTIN, KING
Fourth Row—BUNCH, JONES, YOUNG, DICKSON, HICKMAN
Bottom Row—McREYNOLDS, DOAK, STOUT, ANDERSON, SWINEBROAD

One hundred seventy-nine

Press Club

OFFICERS

JOHN S. ANDERSON . . . . *President*
R. H. DAVIS . . . . *Vice-President*
GLADYS PEELER . . . . *Secretary*

STUDENT PUBLICATION COUNCIL
Student Members

CARL R. YOUNG	JOHN S. ANDERSON	MAYDELL WALLACE	PAULINE CURRY
FRED C. HUGHES	GLADYS PEELER	RALPH PATRICK	CLARA COX
	R. H. DAVIS	BERTHA STOCKARD	

Faculty Members

W. N. MASTERS	MISS MYRTLE E. WILLIAMS	MRS. ELEANOR H. GIBBS
MISS MARY C. SWEET	MISS MARIE E. PHILLIPS	MISS CORA E. STAFFORD
MISS RUBY C. SMITH	MISS CLARA E. MORLEY	MISS MAMIE E. SMITH

YUCCA STAFF

CARL R. YOUNG	ETHEL BUNCH	LEON TALIAFERRO	LOUISE SMITH
CLIFTON C. DOAK	GLADYS PEELER	EXA MINTER	EDITH MARTIN
THYRA WATSON	INEZ JONES	SABRA PARSONS	RUBY GRACE DICKSON
DAN MCALISTER	HELEN EMBERSON	EFFIE MAE CASH	GRACE HOLLOWAY
JACK GALE	JOE HICKMAN	TAYLOR CASH	EUGENE WILKINS

CAMPUS CHAT STAFF

FRED C. HUGHES	JIMMIE JENKINS	R. H. DAVIS	CHARLES LANGFORD
W. L. MURRAY	W. V. LEMMENS	MATTIE MAE THAGGARD	RUTH CRAWFORD
BERTA MAE LOONEY	ELIZABETH ADAMS	C. A. DAVIS	VIVIAN SIMPSON
GLEN O. BALCH	ETHEL BUNCH	C. C. DOAK	FLOIS CRUMP
	R. E. BREWSTER	EUGENIA HENDERSON	

BUSINESS MANAGERS OF PUBLICATIONS

JOHN S. ANDERSON . . . . . *Business Manager*
FRITZ HUMPHREYS . . . *Assistant Business Manager*

CLASS REPRESENTATIVES

BERTHA STOCKARD	. . *Senior*	CLARENCE JOHNSTON	. . *Freshman*
HELEN EMBERSON	. . *Junior*	BILL PATTERSON	. *Second Year*
J. B. DRAKE	. . *Sophomore*	JANIE MAE PATTERSON	*First Year*

Fine Arts Club

Miss Cora E. Stafford, *Club Leader*

OFFICERS

Sabra Parsons . . . . *President*
Lucile Clinkscales . . . . . . *Vice-President*
Exa Minter . . . . *Sec'y-Treasurer*
Annie Cooper . . . . *Campus Chat Representative*

ROLL OF MEMBERS

J. M. Roady	Alice Holman
Myrtle Davidson	Meddie Bice
Theo. Bagwell	Gladys Wilbanks
Louise Smith	Effie McLeod
Mildred Douglas	Exa Minter
Mrs. J. N. Simmons	Lucile Clinkscales
Louise Davidson	Lillian Shipp
Margaret Cannon	Sabra Parsons
Emily Hays	Annie Cooper

Faculty-Student Council

Top Row—W. L. Murray, W. C. Blankenship, J. W. Beaty, J. A. McDonald, F. V. Garrison, Onas Brown
Bottom Row—J. H. Leggett, Mrs. Ross Compton, Maydell Wallace, Mignonette Spillman, Bessie L. Shook, R. H. Davis

OFFICERS

W. C. Blankenship . . . . . *President*
Bessie L. Shook . . . . . *Secretary*

OFFICERS OF STUDENT MEMBERS

R. H. Davis . . . . . . *President*
Maydell Wallace . . . . . *Secretary*

During the Session 1921-22, the Faculty-Student Council has been of invaluable service to the North Texas State Normal College. An entirely new set of rules governing the student body were drawn up by this Council and adopted by the student body.

The Council, which was organized this term, is the foundation for a co-operative plan between the students and faculty of the college to carry on the administration of the college.

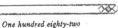

The yucca 1922

The Athletic Council

THE COUNCIL

Top row—St. Clair, Cooper, Maxey, Langford, McDonald
Bottom row—Broadfoot, Thaggard, Doak, Owens, Harris

OFFICERS

C. C. Doak	*President*
J. A. McDonald	*Vice-President*
Ina Owens	*Secretary-Treasurer*
Clyde Cooper	*Business Manager Boys Athletics*
Leonard Maxey	*Ass't Business Manager Boys Athletics*
Queen Thaggard	*Business Manager Girls Athletics*
Charles Langford	*Yell Leader*

This year the Athletic Council has rendered invaluable service in handling the business of the athletic teams, providing for the football banquet, giving a name to the athletic teams which represent the North Texas State Normal College, raising money for the blankets, and otherwise aiding in turning out a championship team during the first season the Normal College was in the T. I. A. A.

A. E. F. Club

OFFICERS

Fall Term		Winter Term	
J. A. McDonald	*President*	Bill Cooper	*President*
Carl R. Young	*Vice-President*	John Hansard	*Vice-President*
W. L. Murray	*Sec'y-Treasurer*	Chas. J. Neely	*Sec'y-Treasurer*
C. A. Davis	*Campus Chat Reporter*		

ROLL OF MEMBERS

Miss Evalina Harrington, *Intercollegiate Canteen Unit, 33rd Division*

E. L. Anderson, *Y. M. C. A.*
Clarence Brown, *36th Division*
Bill Cooper, *Naval Aviation*
C. A. Davis, *34th Division*
Frank Dupree, *7th Division*
J. J. Grace, *16 Co. 3rd Reg., Air Service*
S. B. Graham, *Coast Artillery Corps*
John Hansard, *90th Division*
Fred C. Hughes, *36th Division*
H. R. Jarnegan, *36th Division*
Frank Johnston, *36th Division*
A. J. Landreth, *36th Division*
M. L. Lansford, *36th Division*
Eugene McCloud, *8th Inf. A. S. C.*
J. A. McDonald, *U. S. S. Charleston*

Bert McDuff, *6th Marines*
C. L. Mullins, *U. S. S. Pennsylvania*
W. L. Murray, *7th Division*
C. J. Neely, *U. S. S. Mongolia*
J. F. Norris, *36th Division*
Clellan Overcash, *34th Division*
H. A. Perryman, *2nd Division*
Ector Roberts, *6th Marines*
Stanley Roberts, *36th Division*
W. H. Sims, *90th Division*
J. S. Smith, *U. S. S. R-18*
Marvin Sweatman, *42nd Division*
John R. Venable, *33rd Division*
Carl R. Young, *36th Division*

A. E. F. Club---Summer Session 1921

OFFICERS

L. W. Johnson . . . . . . President
J. B. Lewis . . . . . Vice-President
Miss Evalina Harrington . . Mess Sergeant

ROLL OF MEMBERS

E. L. Anderson
J. Horace Bass
Cecil Booker
L. B. Cooper
C. A. Davis
Tom Gates
Miss Evalina Har-
   rington

Fred C. Hughes
E. O. Hutcheson
E. B. Hutson
H. H. Wellborn
Bill Strong
H. R. Jarnegan
L. W. Johnson
John B. Lewis

J. A. McDonald
J. Frank Norris
W. H. Sims
A. R. Stephens
T. L. Stewart
L. F. Taylor
Carl R. Young
J. C. Penny

1922

Silver Stripers Club

OFFICERS

First Term

H. T. HAYES . . . . President
CLINT WILKS . . . . Secretary

Second Term

C. L. CALDWELL . . . . . . President
D. B. HOKETT . . . . . . Secretary

ROLL OF MEMBERS

C. L. CALDWELL	RALPH PATRICK
E. M. CONNELL	A. V. PRICE
DEAN DAVIS	BEN ROBERTS
R. H. DAVIS	H. L. ROPER
C. C. DOAK	J. W. ST. CLAIR
T. J. FOUTS	HOMER WEEKS
L. L. FRITZ	CLINT WILKES
H. T. HAYES	A. M. WILSON
D. B. HOKETT	V. SMITH
W. M. V. LEMENS	

Choral Club

MISS VALERIE REEVES	*Director*
MISS VIVIAN HUFFAKER	*Accompanist*

OFFICERS

MRS. LULU SHOEMAKER	*President*
H. T. HAYES	*Secretary*
VIVIAN SIMPSON	*Campus Chat Reporter*

ROLL OF MEMBERS

Sopranos

JO BISHOP	EDITH VERNON	BERTA MAE LOONEY
MARY JONES	MILDRED CANTRELL	MARGIE MAHARD
ILEEN COMPTON	FRANCES PRICE	ZELMA WHITE
BESS McCOY	LINNIE GREY	LIZZIE MAE GRIZZARD
LORENA PRUNTY	EUGENIA HENDERSON	MARY SLOAN
LILLIAN SLOAN	GOLDIE CULPEPPER	MARY BONER
MATTIE SMITH	VIVIAN SIMPSON	AMMA BORDERS
LORRAINE WILLIAMS	MINNIE JOE MILLER	MARY CRESWELL

Altos

MRS. LULU SHOEMAKER	
WINNIE DEE McREYNOLDS	
PAULINE CURRY	
WYNONA HILL	
ADA BONDS	
LYDA WILKINSON	
JESSIE LEE CATES	
EVALINE DRIVER	

Tenors

ROBERT TAMPKE
W. O. MORROW
FRANK JOHNSTON
CLINT WILKES
J. E. PURVIS
R. H. DAVIS
MARTIN STEVENS
BEN ROBERTS

Basses

W. C. BLANKENSHIP	S. D. ROBERTS	LOUIE SIMPSON
HOMER WEEKS	HUBERT JOHNSON	BILL PATTERSON
CARL R. YOUNG	H. T. HAYES	A. V. PRICE
BILL BAILEY	H. M. HOLLIS	GLEN BRIAN
D. O. FULTON	L. H. SHIPLEY	

Boys' Glee Club

MISS VALERIE REEVES, *Director*
MISS VIVIAN HUFFAKER, *Accompanist*

OFFICERS

Fall Term		Winter Term	
HOMER WEEKS . . . *President*		ULYS KNIGHT . . . *President*	
ULYS KNIGHT . *Vice-President*		ROBERT TAMPKE . *Vice-President*	
A. V. PRICE . . *Secretary*		A. V. PRICE . . . *Secretary*	
BEN ROBERTS . . . . *Campus Chat Reporter*			

ROLL OF MEMBERS

IVAN OLIVER	W. H. OLIVER
LONNIE PRICE	C. A. DAVIS
STANLEY ROBERTS	H. L. PINKERTON
H. A. WEEKS	R. A. TAMPKE
GEORGE LOUGHMILLER	W. W. FLOYD
W. C. BLANKENSHIP	ULYS KNIGHT
BILL BAILEY	F. C. HUGHES
M. STEPHENS	DEAN DAVIS
BEN H. ROBERTS	R. H. DAVIS

Girls Glee Club

OFFICERS

VIVIAN SIMPSON . . . . *President*
RUTH CARTER . . . . . *Vice-President*
JO MILLER
EFFIE MAE CASH } . . *Secretary-Treasurer*
BLANCHE GARBER
HAZEL HAYES } . . *Sergeants-at-Arms*
MATTIE MAE THAGGARD . . *Chat Representative*

ROLL OF MEMBERS

MABLE ALLEN	BLANCHE GARBER	ELMO NAUGLE
BESSIE ANDREWS	ALMA HATLEY	ELLEN PAXTON
DOLLY BOWEN	WINONA HILL	VIVIAN SIMPSON
ETHELYN BENTLEY	VIVIAN HUFFAKER	FRANCES SIMS
EFFIE MAE CASH	HAZEL HAYES	MABLE SWAFFORD
MILDRED CANTRELL	NORMA HARNESBERGER	ELLEN SIMPSON
NINA DOUGLAS	BARBARA KOON	LOIS TUNNEL
EVELYN DAWSON	LOTTIE KINCANNON	RUTH THOMASON
EVELYN DRIVER	LOIS LOWRIE	MARIE TAYLOR
GENEVIEVE DERRYBERRY	RUTH LILLY	MATTIE MAE THAGGARD
GRACE GARNER	JO MILLER	LELA WOODRUFF
	ODELL MARTIN	

Young Women's Christian Association

MISS SALLIE M. PINCKNEY, *Student Life Secretary*

OFFICERS

CLARA COX	*President*	MARY ALICE UNDERWOOD		*Secretary*
PANSY VARNELL	*Vice-President*	ENIE BESS CARLTON		*Treasurer*

SENIOR CABINET
Chairmen of Committees

BERTHA STOCKARD	*Rooms*	EMILY HAYS	*Hospitality*
JIMMIE JENKINS	*Publicity*	EUGENIA HENDERSON	*Religious Meetings*
LILLIAN ELDER	*Poster*	VIVIAN HUFFAKER	*Music*
HELEN EMBERSON	*Finance*	BERTA MAE LOONEY	*Student Volunteer*
VALA FULLINGIM	*Social*	RUTH CARTER	*Social Standards*

JUNIOR CABINET OFFICERS

CATHERINE MAXWELL	*President*	MARY ELIZABETH WRIGHT	*Secretary*

Chairmen of Committees

FLORENE VANDIVIER	*Membership*	MILDRED DEVENPORT	*Social*
LOUISE BUTLER	*Hospitality*	RUTH CRAWFORD	*Religious Meetings*
WELTA ANGEL		World Fellowship	

1922

Young Men's Christian Association

OFFICERS
1921

W. V. Lemens	*President*
Thomas Davis, Jr.	*Secretary*

1922

J. A. McDonald	*President*
Hugh Colley	*Secretary*

ROLL OF MEMBERS

W. C. Blankenship
Norris Brown
Chas. H. Bryant
Hugh Colley
E. M. Connell
Thomas Davis, Jr.
Chawncy Ford
Lonzo Fort
L. L. Fritz
Hubert Johnson
Philip King
Ulys Knight
W. V. Lemens

L. K. Maxey
Levi Martin
W. L. Murray
Olive McCloud
J. A. McDonald
M. D. McGaughey
C. J. Neely
Ralph Patrick
W. R. Scott, Jr.
C. B. Smith
V. T. Smith
Carrol Wilson

Kindergarten-Primary Club

Miss Evalina Harrington . . . *Leader*

OFFICERS

Mrs. Mabel Simmons . . . . *President*
Pearl January . . . . *Vice-President*
Bessie Alice Kuhn . . . . *Secretary-Treasurer*
Ruth Crawford . . . . . . *Campus Chat Representative*

ROLL OF MEMBERS

Mabel Allen	Mrs. Louise Davidson	Edith Martin	Mrs. Elsie Sprinkle
Mary Alston	Minnie Dearing	R. Inez Meador	Kate Swafford
Lucy May Augustine	Jo Lee Dickson	Verna McGlothlin	La Una Swafford
Estelle Austin	Inez Evans	Olga Odom	Bonnie Taylor
Pearl Badger	Blanche Garber	Sallie Pearson	Florence Terry
Starr Bayless	Corrine Gibson	Ina Pierce	Lucy Tomlinson
Otis Benham	Ruth Gray	Emma Pryor	Rena Mae Waggoner
Ruth Lee Bomer	Leland Gunter	Bess Riddell	Mary Clyde Walker
Essie Ball	Norma Harnesberger	Elizabeth Shrader	Mary Walshak
Muril Boner	Lydia Hendricks	Julia Stafford	Naomi Walshak
Addie Brawner	Bess Herren	Hattie Stark	Gladise Wainscott
Gladys Brian	Olive Jackson	Tommie Stark	Elvera Webb
Mabel Brown	Aetna Jones	Bertha Starr	Mrs. H. Wilson
Kathryn Buie	Mary Jones	Mrs. Bertie Street	Iris Nancy Wood
Lota Fay Burnett	Valda Jones	Alice Strickland	Adelaide Young
Grace Caldwell	Berta Keeley	Lena Strother	Jennie Young
Kathlyn Crawford	Viola Loveless	Gladys Simpson	Alice Yowell
Ruby Crawford	Nell Lumley	Irma Spence	
Mildred Devenport	Lilly Mallow	Effie Springfield	

Educational Exchange

OFFICERS

LEIGH PECK	*President*
C. L. CALDWELL	*Vice-President*
MRS. LULA K. SHUMAKER	*Secretary*

EXECUTIVE COUNCIL

MR. ODAM, *Chairman*	MISS DUGGAN
MRS. COMPTON	R. H. DAVIS
MISS PATRICK	CLARA COX

LEIGH PECK

The Educational Exchange is a professional organization. The Faculty of the Education Department and all students who have had their practice teaching, or who are scheduled for it at any time during the school year, are eligible to membership. The Exchange meets once each quarter. Its purpose is growth in professional knowledge by hearing noted Educators and by publishing educational material.

Faculty Women's Club

OFFICERS

MRS. L. L. MILLER	*President*
MRS. F. V. GARRISON	*Vice-President*
MISS RUTH PARKER	*Secretary-Treasurer*
MISS BESSIE L. SHOOK	*Campus Chat Reporter*

The Faculty Women's Club is primarily a social organization which meets the first Tuesday of each month. At this time the women of the Faculty and the wives of Faculty members meet for recreation and social pleasure, the program being under the direction of several hostesses.

This club is affiliated with the Denton Federation of Clubs, whose aim is civic improvement and the furthering of the interests of the Denton Colleges, as has been shown in the Scholarship gifts to each college.

The Faculty Women's Club radiates its social atmosphere among the Normal students. The successful annual Halloween Party and Class Teas bear witness to this.

Cooke County Club

Navarro County Club

Van Zandt County Club

OFFICERS

JOHN S. ANDERSON	*President*
ALF A. ALLEN	*Vice-President*
EVELYN DAWSON	*Secretary-Treasurer*

ROLL OF MEMBERS

ALF A. ALLEN
JOHN S. ANDERSON
MRS. N. W. ANDREWS
HALLIE BAKER
GRACE BECK
DEANE D. BAILEY
ONAS BROWN
W. F. BROWN
HIRAM BRANDON
EULA BRANDON
HENRYETTA CARTER
RUTH CARTER
CARL DARNELL
EVELYN DAWSON

EVALINE DRIVER
VIRGINIA DUNN
JULIA DURRELL
MATTIE LAND DURRELL
A. D. GAY
HERMAN GAY
N. D. GEDDIE
KATHLYN GRAY
JALENE GRAY
LUCILLE HARDEGREE
LELAND S. HARDEGREE
LORENA HUMPHREYS
H. L. JORDAN
BURON McKIBBEN

LORENA McMAHAN
OLGA MAE ODOM
WENDELL H. OLIVER
MRS. K. PEEKE
HARRY L. PINKERTON
ETHEL SCOTT
ETHEL STUART
LOIS TUNNEL
WHITE TUNNEL
MABEL WALTERS
A. M. WILSON
CARROLL WILSON
JANETTE WILSON

Van Zandt Co. Basketball Team

Top row—DEAN BAILEY, *forward;* ONAS BROWN, *guard;* FRANK BASS, *forward.*
Front row—JESSE RHODES, *guard;* J. F. JORDAN (Capt.), *center.*

History of the Team

ONE of the most interesting features of the Summer School was a county basketball tournament which Mr. St. Clair organized during the first weeks of the Summer Session. The tournament was open to all counties of the State, and six strong rival teams were put in the field. In the preliminaries Denton won over Palo Pinto, and Van Zandt won by a heavy score over Fannin. There is nothing to be said about this game except that Van Zandt had their opponents clearly outclassed at every point.

In the semi-finals, Van Zandt was pitted against the overpowering Parker quintet. The odds were three and four to one favoring Parker, but Van Zandt promptly upset the "dope" and won by a comfortable margin. Rhodes and Brown distinguished themselves at guard. Bailey was the biggest scoremaker. Bass played a good game at forward, and occasionally brought the crowd to its feet with his long shots. Jordan was dealing misery all along the line, and amused himself by dropping the ball through the basket when needed.

The next game was the championship game with Denton. Again the odds were four or five to one on Denton. Denton had two "T" men and otherwise a strong line-up. The final result of the game was in doubt at all times; only the final whistle decided it. Van Zandt won by a margin of four points. Rhodes and Brown at guards held the fast Denton forwards to almost no points. Jordan was here and there, rescuing the ball, and scoring goals at critical points. Bass and Bailey were always delivering goals in pinches. Critics declare the game was of the college type, and that it would take a good college team to beat the Van Zandters.

C. C. Club

FACULTY SUPERVISORS

Miss Lena M. Charter   Miss Edna St. John
Miss Pearl A. Cross

OFFICERS

Ota Belle McCain	*President*
Maydell Wallace . . .	*Secretary-Treasurer*
Ruth Carter	*Campus Chat Reporter*

ROLL OF MEMBERS

Lida Cooper	Ruth Clement	Ethel Bunch
Maydell Wallace	Mae Johnston	Ruby Adams
Berta Mae Looney	Pansy Varnell	Bertha Stockard
Ruth Carter	Ruby Power	Ruth Lynn
Hazel Hays	Emily Hays	Ota Belle McCain
	Rhuey Welch	

MOTTO—LOVE, LABOR, AND LAUGH

For some time the Home Economics girls have longed for an organization of some kind. To meet this need the students and faculty who have lived in the Demonstration Cottage organized the Cottage Cousins' Club, March 4, 1922. As girls enter the cottage they are admitted into the club.

Both the name and the motto are very symbolic of cottage life.

COLLEGE LIFE

Spring Term

San Jacinto Day Celebrated by Spanish Students

SINCE the Texans won every point in the track meet between Texas and Mexico on April 21, 1836, the Mexicans of the Normal College decided not to participate in the field events on Thursday, April 21, 1921. The students voted unanimously to go on a picinic to Club Lake.

For a few moments after meeting, the picnickers stopped in town to purchase "muchas cosas para comer;" then, storing the "eats" on a faithful old truck, the Mexicans began their journey to the scene of enjoyment.

Midway between town and the lake, the truck was no longer faithful. Ique lastima! For a while, no one of the Mexican mechanics seemed to be able to discover the cause of such a display of ill temper, and to secure a truck from town seemed unavoidable. However, by the skill of one of the party, the motor finally resumed its purring and, without further mishap, all reached the lake.

Dos caballeros y una senorita, unable to resist the lure of the water, went in swimming, while the other members enjoyed boat-racing.

Later, because of the fierceness of the elements, the Mexicans were forced to abandon the fire which they had kindled and resort to a vacant cottage nearby, where fortune seemed to favor them. They found a stove on which they prepared various kinds of "eats." After the feast, these Normal Mexicans busied themselves by exploring all sides of the lake, and visiting the dairy, where the craving for "leche" was satisfied. Once again they returned to the cottage, this time to toast marshmallows, and to witness the tricks of a magician who chanced to be among them. After the secrets of the magic had been solved, the Normal Mexicans wended their way back to their southern kingdom.

Interclass Track and Field Meet

The Interclass Track and Field meet at the Normal College on April 28 was an interesting affair and was witnessed by enthusiastic students and visitors.

Those winning first places were as follows:

Boys

Pole vault—Coffman, Sophomore, 9 feet.
High jump—W. West and I. West, Freshmen, tied for first place, 5ft. 7 in.
Broad jump—Cooper, Freshman, 19 ft. 2 in.
Discus—Hooper, second year, 92 ft. 10 in.
120-yard hurdle—J. Hansard, Freshman.
100-yard dash—I. West, Freshman.
220-yard dash—J. Hansard, Freshman.
440-yard dash—B. Hubbard, Freshman.
Half-mile run—F. Hansard, Second Year.
One mile run—F. Hansard, Second Year.

Girls

75-yard dash—J. Thorne, Sophomore
100-yard dash —M. Thorne, Sophomore.
50-yard dash—J. Thorne, Sophomore.
Half-mile walk —Brim, Freshman.
Mile walk—Hicks, Freshman.
60-yard hurdles—J. Thorne, Sophomore.
Basket Ball throw—Ellington, Second Year.
Baseball throw—Ellington, Second Year.
Hop, step, jump—Hicks, Freshman.
High jump—J. Thorne, Sophomore.
Standing broad jump—M. Thorne, Sophomore.
Running broad jump—M. Thorne, Sophomore.

Final Totals of Classes

Girls—Sophomore, 61; Freshman, 17.
Boys—Freshman, 59; Second Year, 41.

Individual Points

Girls—Jonnie Thorne, 23; Margie Thorne, 23; Amber Dean West, 9.
Boys—I. West, 18; John Hansard, 13; Frank Hansard, 10.

A THORN AMONG THE ROSES

The Sophomore Party

IT HAPPENED that the night of May 3, 1921, was blessed with a most glorious moon, which cast a mellow glow for the young of every clime. At our own sheltered little school, the reading rooms were thrown open for the entertainment of the Sophomore Class. The affair was called the Sophomore party; however, that name falls far short of the whole truth. It was much more than a party. It was an event.

The entertainment was of such a nature as to appeal to every type of individual. There were beautiful young women, gay young men, and spacious halls, elaborately decorated and softly illuminated. There was soft music, and lithe young dancers in dainty costumes flitted in and out among the shadows. Their very movements seemed to typify the spirit of youth and joy. All space seemed permeated with just such an atmosphere as would delight the heart of Cupid himself.

In a screened haven sparkling drinks were dispensed, and crystal glasses were alternately filled and drained. There were tables with cards and dice, and eager youth played in reckless forgetfulness of what the world might think. There were shadowy corners with many paired lovers in retreat. Alas! will the world ever offer such another revel as the SOPHOMORE party!

Fair reader, if you are still possessed of the fires of youth, by all means read no farther, but if they have died within you please continue.

For fear that some Soph's mother may be shocked at this account, we will take the space to explain that the foregoing was written before the fickle young author had regained his equilibrium. The dances were of the aesthetic type, and were creditably done by Misses Thelma Clements and Jewell Hooper assisted by four tiny tots; the drinks consisted of fruit punch; the cards belonged to the game called flinch and the dice to "bunco;" the lovers held hands in a game of "Tu Skew;" while the lights were dimmed only while the fairy dancers flitted in the artificial moonlight. On the whole, it was a sane affair supervised by competent chaperones. Oh! how the imagination of youth distorts things!

Now, mothers, don't you feel better?

Wise County Visitors

The N. T. S. N. C. was the host Thursday afternoon, May 12, 1921, to six hundred of the most progressive citizens of Wise County. Public school children, parents, and county officials came to Denton in one hundred cars to spend the day inspecting the two State schools.

Our visitors, arriving on the campus at three o'clock, were met by a guard of honor composed of A. E. F. men in uniform. To the martial strains of the

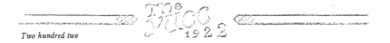

college band, hundreds of visitors passed to the auditorium, where one thousand students and faculty members welcomed them.

Since Dr. Bruce was attending the annual meeting of the Board of Regents, Mr. J. W. Smith presided. Mr. E. D. Criddle made the welcome address. Several ex-Wise County people connected with the Normal and some of the visitors made short talks. Following these was a program given by the Training School.

Since it was then four o'clock, practically no classes were in progress for the visitors to observe; so the A. E. F., Silver Stripers, and others conducted the guests over the campus and through the nine buildings.

In a shady campus nook, punch and ice cream were served by the Y. W. C. A. and the Faculty Club.

The visit of this great number of citizens of Wise County was a most enjoyable and inspiring occasion to the school, to the visitors, and to the town people.

A. E. F. Club Plays

"The Visit of Obadiah," a comedy presented by the A. E. F. Club on April 29, 1921, is long to be remembered and laughed over by the large crowd present.

The actors were all girls from the A. E. F. Club, some of whom, as a result of the makeup, could hardly be distinguished from real feminine actresses; and although the boys were a little awkward at first, they soon became accustomed to the high-heeled shoes and other paraphernalia that belong to the fairer sex. Even Dr. Bruce was charmed by one of the fascinating young ladies and lamented very much when he learned that the girl was a commission doughboy, an ex-buck private in the army.

Following "The Visit of Obadiah," came the "Battle of Rollin' Bones," a negro comedy. The title suggested fun, and the whole was fun.

As the curtain rose, a troop of negroes were seen on the front battling with dice, a natural and favorite pastime with the race. While they were intensely interested in the game, bombs and shells began to fall all around them, showing that the players were more interested in the "battle of bones" than in the real battle.

This little play was a succession of humorous situations such as those common among the negro soldiers. The boys, all having had experience in the army and being familiar with the negro soldier, were able to make their characterization a glorious success.

Yucca Staff Election

CLOSE observers declare this Yucca Staff election to be the best one yet in many respects.

At first, it seemed as if the Lees were to have the field entirely to themselves, but it was not long before prominent Regans and Reagan supporters were seen earnestly talking together.

The new party which grew out of these talks and which was organized by a convention of two representatives from each club in school was called the Student Party. The natural outgrowth of the organization was the ticket of the Student Party.

The election was striking in many details. Flashing cartoons that rivaled Nast and Knott showed that the Lees considered the Student ticket merely a "camouflaged" Reagan ticket. Reagans and Reagan sympathizers argued with equal fervor that the student body had a right to put out a ticket of its own. Both parties advertised with colors, cartoons, and other things and thoroughly aroused the entire college.

J. Horace Bass in chapel briefly stated the position and ability of the Lee candidates, while Lee Preston in his speech pled for the student ticket controlled by the student body.

The Lees based their victory on open politics and the ability of their candidates. The Student Party lost because it was not well represented.

The results were as follows:

	Lees ·		Student Party	
Editor-in-Chief	CARL R. YOUNG	256	J. R. PIRTLE	165
Associate Editor	FRED C. HUGHES	208	C. C. DOAK	218
College Life	OLGA STANLEY	237	VA RUE ORNDORFF	189
Athletics	DAN MCALISTER	254	HARRY PINKERTON	170
Classes	THYRA WATSON	246	ERA JACKSON	180
Facts and Follies	INEZ JONES	210	TEXANNA WILKERSON	176
Art	DOROTHY MILLS	253	LAURA BEARD	173
Organizations	CLARA COX	217	JOHN HINES	208

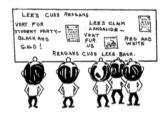

IRIS

DAD AND PEGGY

ONA

JOHNNIE

ROUND ONE

ALTA VISTA

SEVEN!

COME ON OVER

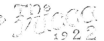

1922

A. E. F. Advance Lines and Take Objective

THE MEMBERS of the A. E. F. and the Silver Striper Clubs, with their lady friends as guests, made the annual hike to the Anderson Farm.
The bugler sounded "assembly" at 1:30, and in a few minutes the defenders of democracy and suffrage "fell in" at the south entrance of the Administration Building, with "Rear Admiral" Neely in command. A "council of war" was held, and it was decided to take on as guide a Frenchman, Monsieur Anderson, captain of the French Zouaves, being chosen to lead the advancing column. This efficient guide showed his contempt for roads, and, to the disconcerting of farmers and their wives along the route, led a direct course across fields, fences and trenches.

When the objective was finally reached, "Major General" Evalina Harrington assumed command, and soon had camp struck near a beautiful little spring. It was gratifying to note the absence of the ever-familiar French sign, "Eaunon potable" about the spring. Numerous fires were going, and the inexperienced were initated into the art of sandwich making, since it was necessary for each one to be his or her own cook. Supper over, the bugler sounded "fall in," and the entire company stood at "attention" for "retreat." "Top Kick" Brewer found it impossible to preserve order and to prevent talking in the ranks with one-half the number girls.

After "retreat" the company engaged in "African dominoes" and various other old army stunts and games. At this time it was reported that "Private" Hughes, who had for some time been A. W. O. L., had been brought into camp. A "court-martial" was ordered, and the accused was defended by "Admiral" Neely and "Lieutenant" Hansard, who attempted to prove his innocence by introducing Miss Elise Haywood and Miss Allie Norwood as witnesses. The prosecution, headed by "Major" Doak, vigorously contended for every inch of the ground, and as is always the case in an army court-martial, the defendant was found guilty. Sentence was pronounced, and the defendant was punished by being compelled to make a public "proposal" to one of the witnesses who had attempted to prove his innocence.

The return home was made without the enthusiasm that marked the outgoing march. The "weary walking wanderers" reached home with the end of a perfect day.

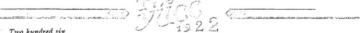

Press Club Banquet

ABOUT fifty members of the Press Club gathered in the Manual Arts Building on the evening of May seventeenth to enjoy the delicious feast arranged for them. The table, decorated in lavender and pink, extended the length of the corridor of the Manual Arts Building, and the delicious menu was in every way worthy of the Home Economics Department.

Toastmaster Hughes made the evening pass quickly by telling jokes on after-dinner speeches. Every one present enjoyed Mr. Wellborn's poem to his typewriter, Mr. Young's 3 a. m. dreams of the Yucca, and Miss Hornbeak's Monday night vision of the Campus Chat. Mr. Masters gave a short talk on the history of the Normal College before it was born twenty years ago, while Dr. Bruce, in his speech, caused those present to realize the future possibilities of the students' publications.

THE ALUMNI BANQUET

The Alumni Association of the North Texas State Normal College has been, since it came into existence, an active and loyal factor in furthering the interests of the college.

Each year during the spring Commencement exercises the Alumni Banquet is held. The banquet of 1921 was one of the best the association has ever had. It was the happy meeting ground of many old-time friends. Ex-students of the Normal from all parts of Texas as well as from other states took advantage of this opportunity to meet, and all had one more good time together.

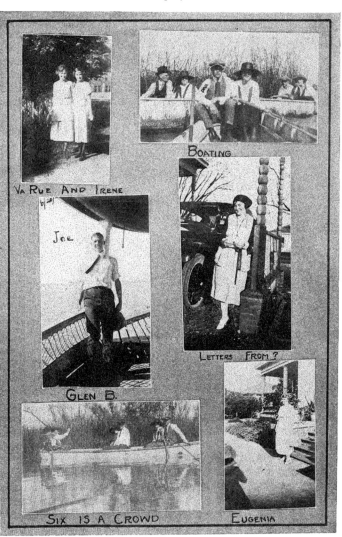

Va Rue And Irene

Boating

Joe

Glen B.

Letters From ?

Six is a Crowd

Eugenia

Dramatic Club Sunrise Breakfast

May 19, 1921, was a gay time for the Lillie Bruce Dramatic Club members, alumni, and friends. The crowd was to be gathered in front of the Library at five o'clock, but of course one need not expect a group of sleepy heads at such an hour. Regardless of hour, when, and where, just before sunrise, two trucks, loaded with a delegation of happy boys and girls and eats to accommodate them were on the way to Club Lake.

The Lake was reached a little after sunrise, and then boat riding and swimming were sought. After an hour and a half of such sport was enjoyed, a breakfast of bacon, eggs, bread and coffee was heartily acceptable. Since the cooking performance had to be gone through with, the campfire was surrounded by many cooks of different classes, ranks and tastes, proud to be the center of action. After several courses of eggs and bacon were served, the ice cream was opened. Even after each person had had several helpings, it was found impossible to use up the supply; so promise of another course later was given.

About nine o'clock, the crowd boarded the trucks and started for home, singing most of the way. At the end of the journey another course of ice cream was enjoyed. Then the breakfasters said goodbye, knowing that from that time on many would meet only like ships that pass in the night winding their way to different shores.

Mary Arden Reception

The reception at Miss Clark's home, on May nineteenth, marked the close of a very successful year for the Mary Arden Club. It was an especially joyous occasion for everyone, not only because all the members of the session of 1920-21 were present, but also because the second "Home Coming" in the history of our school had caused a great many Mary Ardens of former years to be present.

When everyone had arrived, we formed a circle and sang "Auld Lang Syne." Then Mrs. Martin asked that each member step into the center of the circle as his date was called. Each year, beginning with 1907, was well represented.

After the refreshments of dainty cakes and punch had been served, the girls wandered out on the porch, talking of their plans for the future. Some were saying goodbye forever, others were going to teach, and a few were going to be in school again. Just before departing, the members of the Club presented Miss Clark with a silk parasol.

Prunella

The Sophomore Class, in planning for their annual play, hit upon the novel idea of giving it on the lawn. They decided to present 'Prunella," a charming little fantasy, on Friday evening, May twenty-seventh.

Accordingly, a quaint little Dutch house, very prim and "with its eyes shut as if waiting to die," and around it a quainter garden, bounded by high hedges, were constructed. In the center of the garden was a statue of the God of Love, a most important character. Here it was that Prunella, a sweet, unsophisticated girl, played by Miss Dorothy Mills, lived with her aunts, Prim, Privacy, and Prude. Here it was, also, that she first saw the mummers, a band of wandering players. She was captured by Pierrot, chief of the mummers, a part taken by Mr. William Sherrill. In the second act, Prunella, by the thrilling elopement in which Pierrot was assisted by his faithful servant, Scaramel, Mr. Carl Young, left her sheltered garden, and was changed from a simple Dutch maiden to Pierette.

Years afterwards, when Pierrot and Pierette had parted because of Pierrot's wandering nature, and because, as he said, she did not wait long enough for him, they met again in the garden then sadly overgrown and deserted. Their slumbering love was reawakened thru the magic strains which were wafted from the bow of the God of Love.

This happened at the dress rehearsal. For about thirty minutes before the time to start, a near-tempest of wind and rain swept down, sending the spectators scurrying for shelter and the director and players rushing to save the perishable properties.

Mary Arden Carnival

The Mary Arden Carnival came to the Normal Campus in the spring. This Grand Carnival far exceeded any that had ever been in the city of Denton.

One of the most attractive numbers was the Troupe of Russian Dancers with Charles Langford as solo dancer.

Another sensational number was "Wild Nell," a thrilling western story. Those who are fond of bloody combats were especially pleased with this, but for those who appreciate the higher arts, the selection given by Vesta Watson, Grand Opera singer, was perhaps the best feature of the entire program.

Five cent throws at the nigger babies, punches for candy and— It came up a shower of rain about that time and, as I had a crepe paper dress, I had to go home.

Twentieth Anniversary Commencement Exercise

Thursday, May 26

8:30 P. M.....................Concert.

Friday, May 27

9:00 A. M....................Exhibits by the Different Departments.
6:00 P. M....................A. E. F. Club Banquet.
7:30 P. M....................Lawn Fete.
8:30 P. M....................Class Play.

Saturday, May 28

6:00 A. M. to 9:30 A. M......Dramatic Club Breakfast at Club Lake.
10:30 A. M. to 12:00 A. M.....Mary Arden Party at the Home of Miss Clark.
9:00 A. M. to 11:00 'A. M.....Current Literature Club Party
1:00 P. M....................Kindergarten Luncheon.
3:30 P. M....................Ball Game.
6:00 P. M....................Alumni Banquet.
8:30 P. M....................Historical Pageant.
10:00 P. M...................Junior Prom.

Sunday, May 29

11:00 A. M...................Baccalaureate Sermon by Dr. C. C. Selecman
of Dallas.
6:00 P. M....................Vesper Service.

Monday, May 30

9:30 A. M....................Commencement Address by Hon. C. C. Hatchett, Okla. Awarding of Certificates and
Diplomas and Conferring of Degrees.

May 28-29

Home Coming Days.

EXHIBIT DAY

Friday, May 27, 1921

9:00-12:00 A. M.—2:00-5:00 P. M.

Agriculture ⎫
Biology ⎬...Science Bldg.
Botany ⎪
Chemistry ⎭

Drawing..Library Bldg.

Home Economics ⎫
Manual Training ⎬...................................Manual Arts Bldg.
Commerce ⎭

Training School ⎫....................................Education Bldg.
Education ⎭

Commencement Day

The day long looked for by the College—the doubtful day of the First and Second Years, the expectant day of the Freshman, the hopeful day of the Sophomores, the cherished day of the Juniors, and the triumphant day of the Seniors—came as May 30th.

The occasion was unique in that it marked the twentieth anniversary of the College and was hailed by the alumni everywhere as the great "home-coming" day. Ex-students who had not met since leaving the College years before greeted each other with a firm clasp of the hand and a welcome "How's the boy?"

Amidst hearty laughs and exultant voices the various groups which had assembled gathered, as in days past, in the auditorium, where, in eloquent terms, Hon. C. C. Hatchett of Durant, Oklahoma, gave the Commencement address.

Dr. Bruce then awarded those deserving such recognition with certificates and diplomas. After a beautiful eulogy to the Senior class Dr. Bruce presented these soon-to-be alumni with the highest mark of distinction that can be given by the College—the Bachelor's degree.

"Daises Won't Tell"

Summer Recreation

A Quartet

Keep off the Grass

Summer Term

Y. W. C. A. Get-Acquainted Party

NEVER in the history of the Normal College had such a large crowd gathered on the College Campus as the one which came to the get-acquainted party on the night of June 11, 1921. Students from practically every county in the state and from several other states were present at this gay party. It was truly a meeting of the east and the west, of the north and the south, and the mixing and mingling of all in one.

Each student was asked to wear a slip of paper with his name and county written on it. Two students from "Dripping Springs" attracted much attention. They were "Al. K. Hall" and "Bud Weiser." Dr. Bruce, who wore on the lapel of his coat a tag which read, "I am your Boss," was seen talking to old students and greeting new ones.

After all the students had attempted to read all of the tags on every one, refreshments in the form of ice cream cones were served by the Y. W. C. A. girls.

It seemed to the guests that the party had scarcely commenced ere it was time to retire to the boarding houses. Every one left in a jolly mood and with the outstanding fact in his mind that he had attended the largest "party" he had ever "heard tell of."

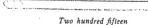

Organization of County Clubs

UNDER the direction of secretary, J. W. Smith, the county clubs were organized about June 20th. Every student in college for the summer session automatically became the member of some county club, and from this time until the close of the term, the clubs were busy going on picnics, watermelon feasts, marshmallow toasts, "wenie" roasts, etc. The roads to Club Lake and Taylor's Lake were traveled many times by truck loads of pleasure seekers, and the demand for picnic trucks was so great on Saturday nights that some clubs were unable to secure transportation to the picnic grounds.

When the gay parties reached the picnic grounds, they enjoyed themselves by making cruises on a nearby lake by means of a few rowboats (minus oars), bathing, playing games and telling jokes and stories.

About an hour before time to return to Denton the club members were called together to enjoy the "feast." Whether it was watermelon, ice cream, "hot dogs" or lunch, you may rest assured that it was greatly enjoyed by all.

Then, as the moon sank behind the wooded hill across the lake, the chaperone would suggest the return to Denton, and the happy couples would clamber aboard the truck and sing old familiar songs on the return journey. Boy! that is what I call LIFE!

SCENE ON CLUB LAKE LAST SUMMER.

A. E. F. Club Convicts Prof. Anderson

ONE of the most sensational charges ever "framed" against a "square man making an honest living" was made against Professor John S. Anderson last summer. The Professor had graciously thrown his house open for the entertainment of the A. E. F. Club, and it came like a thunderbolt from a clear sky when some of the guests brought in "evidence" which proved that officers had been very negligent in the enforcement of liquor laws in Denton.

While Judge Leroy W. Johnson was assembling the court and appointing lawyers, a committee was detailed to search the premises for a "moonshine" still. It is needless to say that this search was fruitless (much to the disappointment of the committee), and all of the "moonshine" they found came from a full moon up in the sky.

Several witnesses were examined by both the state and the defense. The trial was a long, drawn-out affair which would naturally seem to bore the listeners, but did not in this case, because either the jug which contained the "evidence" was stolen by the jury and passed around every five minutes or the judge became so "happy" that he just voluntarily passed it around.

Many facts were brought out concerning the mysterious prowlings of Prof. Anderson with his bottles, and things began to look dark for the defendant because his wife testified against him. Much of the evidence of the male witnesses was ruled out by the judge because they had "sampled" the "evidence" too freely, and it seemed that they couldn't remember very well.

The case was brought to a dramatic climax when the judge instructed the jury to return a verdict of guilty. The jury did this and warned the Professor that he must increase the capacity of his still and improve the quality of the "milk." Besides this he was sentenced to propose to the judge's wife. The judge immediately suspended the last clause in the sentence. Thus Professor Anderson has a suspended sentence hanging over his head till this day.

Peaches

Who said there was a peach shortage this summer? Either he was not in Denton or he is blind. In either case we are sorry for him.

First of all we have the irresistible pink-cheeked May peach who is just out of high school and is always in demand. Who wouldn't hang around an orchard (or a boarding house) if there was a possibility of swiping one of these? Then there is the full, round, rosy Elberta of midsummer, sweet and most sought after of all. Lucky is the guy who can pluck one of these. There are a few, though not many, speckled, somewhat wrinkled and, as everybody knows, sour.

There are fresh peaches, green peaches, over-ripe peaches and spoiled peaches, but let us hope, for their sweet sakes, that none of them get "canned" this summer.

Play Hours

The Y. W. C. A. gave the students of the college many happy hours during the summer. One night each week games were played on the campus before curfew. This tended to keep up a fine spirit of fellowship among the students and to form new friendships. It was a turning aside and forgetting the daily toil in class-rooms for a few minutes and was of great benefit to the students.

Numerous games were played and enjoyed by all, and sometimes the Y. W. C. A. girls or a special group of people would put on a stunt for the benefit of the students. Let's have more of it this summer. It provides for innocent amusement and keeps many of us out of mischief.

Silver Stripers Give Bacon Fry

Another live club which was strongly organized during the summer session was the Silver Stripers. It was composed of men who had been in the military service in the late war and who were not assigned to units which went overseas.

This club was royally entertained at the home of Mr. O. L. Davis on the evening of July 2nd. An abundant supply of bacon was brought forth and the guests broiled it over the open fire. Of course there were onions, pickles, mustard and coffee to top off the bacon sandwiches. In fact, old memories of camp life were revived in the minds of the ex-service men.

As soon as the hunger of the guests had been satisfied, they were bidden to gather on the large lawn and indulge in games such as "Jacob and Ruth," "The Flying Dutchman," etc., and it was pleasant to see the guests behave like grammar-school students instead of dignified college men and women.

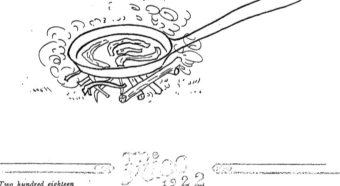

The Baptist Reception

During the early part of the summer session the First Baptist Church of Denton honored the students of the college with a reception. Several hundred students crowded into the basement of the church, which was decorated with green boughs, pot plants and Japanese lanterns.

A large booth occupied the center of the room. From this booth punch was served throughout the evening to the thirsty throng. Different organizations of the church had booths in different parts of the room, and these booths were visited by the guests.

Then a musical program, as well as several short talks by representatives of different organizations of the church, was greatly enjoyed by all.

Art Lectures by Miss Hillyar

Among the many things which the students had in the way of entertainment during the summer session were two very interesting art lectures by Miss Hillyar of the College faculty. These lectures were given on the large lawn near the Manual Arts building, and patient and interested audiences went each time to view the lantern slides as they were thrown on the screen and clearly explained by Miss Hillyar.

The purpose of the lectures was to acquaint the students with the masterpieces of art and architecture beginning with the earliest examples and continuing through the Middle Ages.

Methodist Lawn Party

Mr. and Mrs. T. E. Peters, acting host and hostess for the First Methodist Church, entertained the college students with a delightful lawn party during the early part of the summer session.

After the guests were divided into groups and each group had "pulled a stunt," the big event of the evening was announced. This was the rendering of a number of selections by a male quartette. Hugh Porter added some so-called "specialties" to this. Judge Speer welcomed the students and a cordial invitation was given to attend the Methodist Church while in Denton.

A very original idea was carried out in the method of serving refreshments. The refreshment booth was skillfully built to represent a vine-covered well, and by the light of Japanese lanterns the guests were served with punch throughout the evening.

Dr. Sutton Speaks in Chapel

It was the rare privilege of both faculty and students to hear Dr. W. S. Sutton speak at the chapel hour on July 9th. Dr. Sutton is Dean of the School of Education of the University of Texas.

"Social Problems of the Day," the subject of Dr. Sutton's address, was discussed from three standpoints: the political condition of the nations, the moral condition of society, and the present condition of education. Dr. Sutton handled these topics in a very pleasing manner, and only lack of time prevented him from taking up other problems of great interest to the college student.

Band Concerts

Among the many things that were provided for the entertainment of the summer students in order that life would not be so monotonous, the city band was secured for several concerts. A band stand was erected near the Manual Arts building and electric lights were arranged in such a way that the musicians could easily see the music.

The large audience would entirely surround the band stand and sit on the lawn to listen to the music and to converse in low tones with friends.

All enjoyed these concerts very much and displayed their approval by applauding loudly at the end of each number.

County Basketball Games

Much interest was aroused in the student body when the county clubs organized basketball teams. Some of these were composed of veterans who had made letters on basketball teams at the Normal and other colleges in past years.

Not so much enthusiasm was shown in the preliminary games, but large crowds thronged the campus in the semi-finals and finals. Formidable teams were put in the field by Van Zandt, Parker, Denton and Fannin counties, and the state students. Each team was eliminated until Van Zandt and Denton teams alone remained undefeated. A game was arranged between these two to determine the county basketball champions, and the game proved to be of college caliber from start to finish. Van Zandt finally went ahead the winner in the last few seconds of play, and the final score was 32-30.

The men who composed this championship team were: Bailey and Bass, forwards; Rhodes and Brown, guards, and Jordan, center. Jordan played a cool, deliberate game, and it was a sensational field goal thrown by him which defeated the Denton county team.

The Educational Exchange Organizes

An organization which has meant much to the students of the College is the Educational Exchange, which was established during the summer session. The purpose of the exchange is to keep the members in touch with each other so that first class material may be exchanged after members have gone out to teach. Also prominent educators are secured to make lectures to the exchange, and in this manner students derive valuable information which may be used in their own classrooms later.

Dramatic Club Plays

During the early part of the summer session the Lillie Bruce Dramatic Club organized. The club had good material for a very successful season because many students who had enrolled in the college for the summer session had been members of the club before and had the advantage of experience in dramatic club work.

The plays were given on Monday evening before the curfew bell rang so that the students would be able to attend without using part of the time that should be given to study.

"The Neighbors" was given by the club during the session. The small town atmosphere as created by the different characters was very amusing to the audience.

"Borrowers' Day," "Miss Susan's Fortune" and "The Dear Departed" were other plays which had the small town as their setting. Large audiences greeted these plays, also, despite the fact that the auditorium was very sultry.

Other presentations were: "The Maker of Dreams," on August 8th and "Chrysanthemums," on August 15th. The latter play had a setting quite different from the others, being a Japanese play, and, to say the least, a very charming one.

Faculty Wins Volley Ball Championship

Volley ball games were played every evening after supper on the campus south of the Library. Finally, as the game began to grow in popularity, the classes and Faculty decided to organize teams and arrange a schedule of games. This was done, and it was soon seen that the Faculty and the Freshmen had the strongest teams.

After these two teams eliminated the other class teams, they met for the championship. An enthusiastic crowd was out to root for each and brilliant plays made the observers gasp in wonder. The Freshmen won the first game before the Faculty could get warmed up, but the Faculty drew blood in the second game by winning easily. The Freshmen then rallied and won the third game by four points.

By this time darkness had begun to interfere with the playing and so it was decided to go to the gymnasium and finish the game. As the delay somewhat demoralized the Freshmen team, the Faculty won the fourth game. The two teams were then tied with two games each. Excitement ran high as the Freshmen took the lead in the fifth game, and it looked like a victory for them, but the Faculty rallied when the score was 13-10 against them and swept forward to a sensational victory and the championship.

President of Baylor University Visits Normal

Among the distinguished persons who visited the College during the summer session was Dr. S. P. Brooks, President of Baylor University. It was the privilege of the faculty and students to listen to him deliver a most interesting lecture on "The Many Sidedness of the Character of the Teacher" on the evening of July 26th. His audience was very attentive and appreciative.

Dr. Brooks emphasized the great opportunity which the teacher has for leadership in the community—leadership in educational, religious and social movements, and every good thing which tends to build up the community and make good citizens of the boys and girls who are influenced by them.

A note of patriotism as well as of appreciation of the teacher rang throughout his speech.

Dr. Brooks very fittingly closed his lecture by reading a poem which told of a high cliff over which many people had fallen and had been seriously injured. Finally the community decided to station an ambulance at the foot of the cliff to carry to the hospital the people who were unfortunate enough to fall over. Dr. Brooks made his point by showing that the remedy should have been made at the top of the cliff instead of at the bottom, and that this same principle should be applied to our educational standards. The remedy should be applied to the cause of the weakness of our educational standards, and not to the result.

Interesting Football Game

Coach St. Clair arranged a football game between two groups of students who were taking a course in football coaching during the session. In spite of the exceedingly hot August weather the boys worked out about ten days before the game was to be played.

In a few minutes after the two teams took the field every player was wet with perspiration. To some extent this prevented a fast game.

Neither team was able to score in the first quarter, but Brannon pulled down a forward pass and raced for a touchdown in the early part of the second quarter.

The score stood 6-0 in favor of Brannon's squad until the last play of the game, when Doak received a forward pass and fell across the goal line, thus making the score 12-0 in favor of Brannon's squad. Nevertheless, Tipp's squad played a good brand of football, even if the score stood against them at the end of the game.

The Seniors Go A-Fishing

Yes, the dignified seniors pushed aside their books and hunted up fishing canes, lines, etc., to go a-fishing. And what is more, they caught about thirty-five pounds of fish, enjoyed a big feast and stayed all night.

Of course, sleep was impossible; so the more adventuresome members of the party went frog hunting and brought in some prize catches. The rest of the party contented themselves with hiding the cover and shoes of those who were asleep or trying to sleep.

At last Sunday morning dawned upon the sleepy party and two boys were detailed to cook breakfast for the rest. After much delay the breakfast was served and preparations were made for the journey back to the college. The seniors had many a wild fish story to tell the lower classmen for several days after the trip.

Summer Commencement Exercises

A new feature was introduced into the commencement exercises which were held on Saturday, August 20th. This was the processional which was formed in the library building, and with Dr. Bruce and the Faculty leading, marched into the auditorium. The candidates for degrees, diplomas and certificates followed in order and took seats which had been reserved for them.

The musical program was rendered by the Choral Club, and Dr. Bruce made a very impressive address to the class.

At the conclusion of the address the graduates of the Sophomore Class were presented with permanent certificates and the candidates for degrees were awarded their degrees and diplomas.

The entire faculty wore caps and gowns at this commencement exercise, a custom to be followed at similar exercises in the future.

Studying

All By Myself   Summer House-keepers   Romance

Wm. Herschel and
Lillie Bruce

Gentleman of Leisure

Cold Drinks

Housewives To Be

The Get-Acquainted Party

The Normal Campus was a scene of merriment on Friday evening, October first. Old and new students thronged there to see familiar faces and welcome new ones with whom they were to associate during the coming year. There might have been a half-way forlorn feeling to know that all of the old students were not back again, but the big pleasure of greeting new ones crowded it out.

Not only students, but also a great number of the faculty, gathered there, and all enjoyed the party equally. Why not? Even Dr. Bruce was star actor in a play suggested by Miss Pinckney, the new Y. W. C. A. secretary. There were also several other "stars" in the play, the names of which no one knew until it was all over, and then—Oh, well, why are we all "Nuts?" For the play simply was "Gathering Nuts." The poem, "Curfew Shall not Ring Tonight," was acted out very artistically by a fascinating young lady and two handsome men, while Miss Garrison concealed herself behind a great oak and read the poem effectively. The students were divided into groups according to their birth month, and each group performed a stunt, which was interesting and of course humorous.

Last and best of all were the refreshments, cream cones, served by the Y. W. C. A. Charming Y. W. lassies with prettily decorated containers stood beside the lines of the grand march and served each one as all came by in twos to get their bit.

After the Fire   The Homeless Ones

Corona Maids   Four's A Crowd   Oh, Why Not?

Ye Chemistry Sharks!

A. E. F. Club Party

THE A. E. F. Club, which, since its organization, has been one of the foremost social clubs, held its first meeting of the session at the home of Mr. and Mrs. E. L. Anderson on Saturday evening, October fifteenth.

The old-time bonfire was kindled and soon its glowing flames attracted those who had come for a good time. In a short time each person was preparing his own meat for his sandwiches, which were greatly relished. Coffee also was served, in army fashion, sufficient in quantity to satisfy a whole regiment.

Many out-of-door games were participated in, and that informality which the ex-service man can appreciate better than anybody else caused the guests to feel that it was good to be there.

After all had become tired at these games, the pleasure of the evening was continued from another source. Miss McReynolds gave a reading, which was followed by stories told by Miss Harrington, a reading by Miss Cates, and a talk by Mr. McDonald on "The Contribution of an Old Bachelor to Society."

Those present were Misses Harrington, Edwards, Long, Cash, Cates, McReynolds, Thomas, Christian, Pitman and Creswell, and Messrs. Cook, Hughes, McDonald, Hansard, Bralley, Young, Venable, Davis and Murray.

At a late hour of the night the merry crowd, as 'taps" was sounded, answered its command, expressing appreciation to the host and hostess for a very enjoyable evening.

Mary Arden Reception

The Mary Arden Club, on Monday afternoon, October the seventeenth, at the home of Miss Edith Clark, had its first meeting for the session 1921-1922.

During the business session, roll call was made interesting by each member's responding with her reason for wishing to be a Mary Arden. Needless to say, each and every one of the responses was highly complimentary to the club and to its "Little Mother." Miss Clark, in return, extended a greeting of welcome to each member, old or new.

With Miss Ethel Bunch acting as temporary chairman, the officers for the first term were elected.

An interesting part of the afternoon's program was the "past history" and the "future plans" of the Mary Arden Club as given by Miss Clark, the "Mother of the Mary's," who divulged the secret of a cherished plan to build at some future time a Mary Arden Club House.

During a most delightful social hour spent in getting acquainted, Miss Bessie Shook presided at the punch bowl, while Miss Sallie Pinckney and Miss Janie Duggan assisted in serving fruit punch and stick candy to the club members.

Our Hallow-een Party

ONE OF the most attractive events of the season was the Hallow-een party, sponsored by the Women's Faculty Club, and given by the different organizations of the college on Monday evening, October the thirty-first.

According to custom, every one came masked. There were "spooks" of every description present. The program was opened in the Auditorium by the children of the lower grades of the Training School, who gave the goblin and witch dance. This was cleverly done and was enjoyed by every spook present.

Immediately after this came the Dramatic Club's presentation of a famous wizard of the Hindoos. This character was able to produce, in actual scenes, the past, the present and the future of many members of the Faculty. This was an exceedingly interesting feature of the party, and the crowd was in constant uproar while seeing the revelations of the future.

From the Auditorium the gay crowd scattered to various points of interest on the campus and in the Library, where booths and side shows furnished amusement for the remainder of the evening.

The Lee Literary Society, in connection with the Mary Arden Club, gave perhaps the most spooky feature of the evening. The Reading Room, which was decorated with fantastic colors, contained fortune tellers and such interesting diversions as jobbing for peanuts with hatpins. The major feature of this department, however, was manifest when the curtain was drawn. There stood Satan, with his corps of imps, presiding over a huge pot, around which the flames played merrily; on each side was the graveyard. As the shades slipped up from their tombs at the ghostly hour of midnight, for their annual frolic, they were pounced upon by Satan and tossed into the ghostly flames.

The nerves of the spectators were not calmed when, fleeing from the graveyard scene, they found themselves in a room where Bluebeard was standing guard over a number of wives, who were strung up by their hair and were screaming wildly for help. The screams were rewarded by Bluebeard's tickling their chins.

The entertainment of the Reagan Literary Society and the Current Literature Club introduced a fortune telling witch, a man with a clammy handshake and other side attractions. The main feature was a negro minstrel. This ebony group proved very popular with the crowd, as they sang songs and told jokes. Then the crowd was escorted through the grave diggers' department, provided by the C. L. C. The Y. W. C. A. girls had arranged a very attractive booth at the fountain and were selling apples, cream cones and other refreshments.

A. E. F. Club on a 'Possum Hunt

Wednesday afternoon, November ninth, at 5:30 all members of the A. E. F. Club and their lady friends who cared to chase the sleek tailed-pelt, commonly called the 'possum, were ordered to fall in at the south entrance of the Administration Building. A Ford truck and a Buick touring car met the company there to transport them to a secluded spot on Clear Creek, where they might cook their regulation supper and hunt 'possums if they so desired.

When the purr of the motors had hardly ceased, the underbrush was lighted up by the camp fire. As soon as the fire died down to the point at which it could be safely approached, there was a scramble for weinies and bacon. The appetizing odor of burning grease and cooking coffee soon drew all wood details back into camp, and the feast ensued. Were weinies and bacon all they had to eat? No! There were pickles, coffee, bread and a good supply of pies.

Soon after supper, the company announced its readiness for the hunt. All eyes were turned toward the mess sergeant whose duty it was to provide the dog, but his only announcement was: "I forgot him." Not to be outdone by the mere absence of a dog, Mr. Anderson suggested that the crowd go forth in mass formation and run down the animals without the aid of a canine leader. Then came the wild chase. Down the creek bottom went the crowd, thru briar patches and thick growth of underbrush. It was in this chase that many a fair damsel could be heard to shriek out in vain as she plunged headlong into an entanglement of sharp briars. Some of the damages of this chase were healed by the common use of the needle and thread, but others demanded the slow but sure work of nature.

Time was swiftly passing by and the going through the bottom was hard, but one by one the crowd drifted back to camp, until they were all present or accounted for. Upon closer observation, however, it was noticed that to the very last couple not a 'possum was captured.

Chapel Exercises

On Thursday morning, November tenth, the A. E. F. Club conducted the chapel exercise. Miss Reeves led a number of war songs, which, I am sure, brought pictures of unspeakable horror to the minds of some.

The Reverend Mr. McClung directed the devotional exercise, and the Reverend Mr. Mathieson, pastor of the First Christian Church of Denton delivered an address. The latter speaker, having served in the capacity of chaplain in the British Armies in New Zealand, and also in the same capacity in the American Armies in the past World War, was able to touch the very heart and soul of every man who served in the American Expeditionary Forces.

After the address, a solo rendered by Miss Ousley of the C. I. A. was received with great applause.

Armistice Day Celebrated

At 7:30 o'clock on Friday morning, November eleventh, a large crowd assembled on the campus to commemorate the third anniversary of Armistice Day by raising the flag. As the flag was slowly raised and the bugle was sounded, our minds were drawn from the gaiety of the present celebrations to a sad recollection of the past which made us hope that we shall never again see such destruction of mankind.

At 8:30 the ex-service men of the Normal marched down to the corner of the square and there joined the American Legion detachment. Then, as a unit, they paraded the square, after which they were marched onto the lawn at the west side of the court house, where they remained until the rest of the parade had passed.

After the parade, the ex-service men assembled in the First Christian Church, where the Arthur O. McNitzky Legion Post elected officers for the ensuing year. The men then received their tickets to the banquet served at the First Baptist Church, sponsored by the Women's Federated Clubs of Denton. Prof. E. L. Anderson was master of ceremonies. A welcome address was made by the Reverend S. J. Mathieson, and the response was given by Capt. Clark Ousley. A eulogy to mothers was then delivered by Capt. Newton Rayzor. The orchestra from the College of Industrial Arts furnished the music for the songs and played during the serving of the banquet. The dinner was excellent, and all the ex-service men joined in an expression of appreciation.

Y. W. C. A. Banquet

The Y. W. C. A. banquet, which was held in the Girls' Reading Room on the evening of November nineteenth, was a great success. There had not been such enthusiasm shown this year as was shown that evening by the two hundred girls who were present.

The room was beautifully decorated in green and white, and the entertainment was very lively and interesting, because of the efforts of the toastmistress, Miss Clara Cox. Miss Pansy Varnell gave a toast to the Advisory Board members, which was responded to by a toast to the cabinet members from Miss Shook. Misses Berta Mae Looney, Elizabeth Adams and Helen Emberson, and Mrs. Shumaker gave a "four-dimension" toast, the dimensions being addition, subtraction, multiplication and division, respectively. Miss Stockard made a short talk on the needs of the Girls' Rest Room. Miss Ruth Carter told about the work of the hospitality committee. Following Miss Ruth Crawford's announcement of the vesper services, Miss Helen Emberson discussed the finances of the association. Peppy college songs, led by Miss Mamie Smith, were sung through the evening, and the program was further enlivened by readings by Miss Emberson.

The menu, which was served in two courses, consisted of olives, celery, meat loaf, potatoes, cranberries, white sauce, hot chocolate, ice-cream and cake.

"Sally From the Alley"

"My Blushing Rose"

"The Cameo"

"Snowflake"

"Clarence" Act IV

Dramatic Club Party

The evening of November 11, 1921, will be a memorable one for the members of the Lillie Bruce Dramatic Club. About eight o'clock couples from all over town were assembling at the home of Mrs. Compton on West Hickory Street. They found the beautiful parlor decorated with patriotic colors, lighted by the soft glow of red and blue lights, and warmed by a cheerful fire, awaiting them.

After the guests had heard the music of the Edison for a short time, the social committee led in a number of "peppy" games. The program had been so arranged as to keep every one happily participating at all times.

After awhile everybody was given a pencil and paper and asked to be seated. This was the preparation for another pleasant surprise. Five or six clever charades were given, and the guests guessed what each represented.

The hostess, assisted by the social committee, then served a delicious plate luncheon, in which the patriotic color scheme was carried out.

Beside the regular members, Mrs. Bruce, some former members, and a few out-of-town guests were present.

Junior Party

The Junior Class of the Normal College had one of its most enjoyable socials at the home of Mrs. Ilene Compton. The scene was one of perfect enjoyment for the Juniors.

At seven o'clock the guests were met at the door by the hostess, and immediately the fun began. The social chairman with her committee, had planned the entertainment. Games and diversions of various kinds were in progress during the entire evening. One of the most enjoyable features of the entertainment was the dancing of ye good old Virginia Reel. (No doubt Mr. Weeks will verify the statement.) The music was furnished by the Edison.

The hostess, assisted by members of the social committee, served a delightful plate luncheon consisting of tea, sandwiches and homemade candies.

Needless to say, when the dreaded hour of ten-forty-five came, there were thirty reluctant farewells made. In fact, we were afraid for a time that Miss Clark with all of her forces would have to be called out to teach some people (it wou not do to call names), that ten-forty-five is the end of things for Normalitesld

This party has served to unify the junior class more closely. Armed with "pep" and feeling of true comradeship, there is no limit to what we may accomplish. If you want to be in the happiest best group in school, manage a reclassification and be a Junior.

Act II

Act II

Act I

Act III

Act IV

SCENES FROM "CLARENCE"

Clarence

"Clarence," by Booth Tarkington, was presented by the Lillie Bruce Dramatic Club on November twenty-eighth, with a finesse of artistry rarely found in amateur productions. Throughout the play, the sympathetic audience responded with chuckles, a murmur, a ripple or an uproar of laughter as the rich Tarkington humor, now subtle, now broad, was put over by the players with professional poise, or was tense with excitement as a near-tragic climax struck like a storm cloud in the second act, to be dispelled in the third with the sunshine of the mysterious personality of Clarence.

Clarence was taken by John Anderson in a manner deserving high praise. Carl Young as Mr. Wheeler, overburdened with the cares of a big business and weighed down with the responsibility of a quarrelsome family; Winnie D. McReynolds, as Mrs. Wheeler, second wife of Mr. Wheeler as well as an inexperienced step-mother; and Texana Wilkirson, as Violet Pinney, governess in the Wheeler home, under suspicion by Mrs. Wheeler, each showed interpretative ability in his respective cast. The by-characters, Hubert Stem, by C. C. Doak; Dinwiddie, the butler, by Jack Gale; Della, the maid, by Lorena Humphreys; and Mrs. Martyn, confidential secretary to Mr. Wheeler, by Ethel Bunch, were carefully played. Easily the star of the evening was Helen Emberson, as Cora, the high-tempered, self-willed daughter of the house. Her acting served to portray more vividly the droll humor of the quite Tarkingtonesque character of "Bobby," the young man of the house, "hovering on the elder side of sixteen," a part played by Joe Hickman.

Some effective song specialties were given between acts.

The characteristic stage settings contributed no small part toward the artistic quality of the whole play.

Lyceum Number

The second Lyceum number of the session was a lecture by Mr. Edgar C. Raine, illustrated by pictures. The subject was "Alaska, The Frontier Wonderland of the World," and Mr. Raine knew much about it as he has spent more than twenty years in Alaska and has visited every town and village in that country. Nor was the lecturer unmindful of the value of good jokes, as he related that kind which made the audience laugh with him.

The pictures of the beautiful rivers and snow-covered mountains were very pleasing to the audience, while other pictures caused surprise and amazement. Who expected to see those stately mansions, those towns with street cars, that luxurious growth of various kinds of vegetables, those trucks loaded with people going to a midnight baseball game?

DETOUR, PLEASE

DON'T ANNOY US!

STEADY

LET'S GO.

I HATE TO LEAVE YOU.

THIRSTY?

Musical Club's Barbecue

Any kind of picnic is jolly, of course—but a picnic de luxe, with fireworks, bonfires and barbecue! Ah, shades of old-time merrymakers!

It was the week before Christmas that the Associated Musical Clubs of the College, with Dr. and Mrs. Bruce as honor guests, assembled under a very pleasing yellow moon, ordered especially for the occasion, and betook themselves to the Athletic Park, where a huge bonfire awaited them. Time-honored games were played, while savory odors from the barbecue pit betokened good things to come. Then the guests marched to the "cafeteria," where they were served a delicious supper, of which the piece de resistance was barbecued chicken.

After supper someone discovered apples that grew on oak trees, and a wild scramble ensued to secure specimens of this magic fruit. Then came marshmallow roasting, interspersed with songs. Finally, the picnic ended fittingly with a display of Christmas fireworks.

Christmas Cantata

"Glory to God in the highest; on earth, peace, good will to men."

This was the theme of the old, old story presented by the College Choral Clubs in the sacred cantata, "The Holy Child," by Adams, on Sunday afternoon, December the eleventh, in the college auditorium.

The candle light service in the quiet of vesper hour created an atmosphere of reverent solemnity, which the rendition of the cantata further sustained. Miss Berta Mae Looney, soprano; Mr. Ben Roberts, tenor, and Mr. Robert Tampke, baritone, as soloists, and the men's semi-chorus, all Choral Club members, sympathetically interpreted the narrative of the Savior's birth and

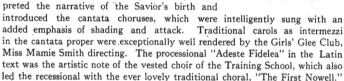

introduced the cantata choruses, which were intelligently sung with an added emphasis of shading and attack. Traditional carols as intermezzi in the cantata proper were exceptionally well rendered by the Girls' Glee Club, Miss Mamie Smith directing. The processional "Adeste Fidelea" in the Latin text was the artistic note of the vested choir of the Training School, which also led the recessional with the ever lovely traditional choral, "The First Nowell."

Most responsive instrumental accompaniments of Messrs. John Cobb, Homer Richey and Floyd Graham, together with the excellent pianistic work of Miss Vivian Huffaker, added much to the artistic ensemble, while the spirit of harmony, peace and good will evidenced in the efforts of the Choral Clubs remained in the hearts of every one afterward to bless the season.

Christmas Reception of Mary Arden Club

The annual Christmas reception of the Mary Arden Club was held on Wednesday evening, December seventh, in the Music hall. The hall was tastefully decorated in holiday colors, and furnished a beautiful background for the very delightful function.

Each guest was given the name of a character from Shakespeare; then Romeo having found his Juliet, and each young man his maiden, everyone entered into the spirit of the evening with an interesting game of conversation. There were vague references made to "the first Christmas tree I could remember," "or what I did last Christmas." All of these topics were very interesting, but when Helen Emberson started telling about how Providence and a nail changed the whole course of a man's life, everyone stopped breathless with suspense (perhaps thinking that he might conceive an idea of changing his future). The reading was artistically interpreted and enjoyed by all the guests. Among other readings given, those by Bill Cooper and Fred Hughes were heartily appreciated.

The true spirit of Christmas was observed in the soft singing of "Holy Night" by everyone present, while only the candles, burning under a large copy of the Madonna, lighted the hall. Later the candles on the Christmas tree were lighted, and the "snowballs" distributed Christmas stockings to the boys. In a contest in identifying silhouettes of men of the Normal College faculty, Ben Pierce and Grace Frazell won the prize.

Refreshments of punch, sandwiches, blanched almonds, mints and cakes were served, closing the program of a most enjoyable evening.

Pleasing Recital at Normal College

The recital of Reed Miller and Navada Van Der Veer at the Normal College was an auspicious opening number of the season's lyceum course. The program was well chosen to display the versatility of the two artists, and featured a number of American composers.

Mme. Van Der Veer's contralto showed remarkable range and power, and proved to be a voice of rich and colorful sweetness. One of her most pleasing numbers was the beautiful aria from "Heriodiade."

Mr. Miller, who is known to Denton music lovers, sang in his usual vigorous style. His voice assumes the poignancy of "Salvation Rosa," the sublimity of "The Living God" or the sheer Irish sentiment of "Bally Bree" with equal ease. The duet from "Jewels of the Madonna" was sung with commendable style, as was the closing number, "Who is Sylvia."

Winter Term

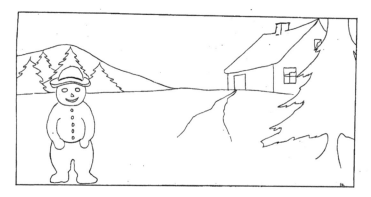

A. E. F. Club

On the night of January seventh, at 6:30, Lieutenant-Colonel McDonald called the forces of the club, accompanied by their friends, to the barracks.

The first thing in order was the election of new officers for the following term; then came games, suggested by Miss Harrington, in which all took part. Later sandwiches were served with boiled eggs and real army coffee. But the mess sergeant seemed to think this was not sufficient; so pie, nuts and other delicacies were added.

At the proper hour the merry circle adjourned, each expressing what a "jolly good" time he had had.

Arthur Middleton Renders Interesting Program

Arthur Middleton, bass baritone of the Metropolitan Opera Company, presented in concert by the Lyceum Committee of the Normal College at the First Baptist Church Thursday evening, January twelfth, attracted a capacity audience, the responsiveness of which further attested to the reputation of this genial American artist.

Mr. Middleton combines with virile personality a vocal organ of extensive range, beauty of quality and unlimited capacity for emotional expression, controlled with a dexterity completely satisfying. The program was well chosen to display the versatility of the singer.

Perhaps he was in his happiest vein in offering the group of Italian numbers, with especial reference to the "Povero Marinar," although the rollicking vivacity of the "Largo al Factotum" from the "Barber of Seville" brought forth a spontaneous and insistent encore.

Mr. Middleton was consistently gracious in responding with encores to each group.

The Sophomore Class Party

O N THE evening of January thirty-first one passing the Barracks would have seen, not a crowd of athletes and pep promoters, but the sophomore class having the best of times. As the members entered, they heard "peppy" music and at once knew that fun had begun.

Soon the anxious groups were ushered to seats near the center of the building, and Miss Louise. Preston entertained them by an example of Terpsichorean art. Then Miss Cates appeared with her hands filled with strings. Each of eight boys was given one end of a string, the other end of which a girl securely held. At a signal each boy pulled his string and found his partner. For five minutes these partners talked. Then each boy described the girl to whom he had talked and each girl wrote the life aims of the boy.

As Mr. Cronkrite informed the merry crowd that the North Pole had suddenly been transferred to this Southland for their benefit, two skaters, Misses Louise Preston and Henrietta Carter, dressed in solid white, appeared before the surprised company and glided swiftly and smoothly across the ice.

Next came the grand march "Across the River," in which all present participated. The marchers proceeded until the music suddenly ceased, at which time several of the couples were asked to "fall out." Why? No one knew. The process continued. At length the one couple remaining was presented with a can opener tied with a bow of pink ribbon. Until then it was not noticed that a large ring was drawn on the floor and that all who stopped within its boundaries were dismissed from the line of march.

The next thing on the program was a quartet by Messrs. Davis, Tampke, Roberts and Blankenship.

But this was not the end. Soon a large tray of gingerbread was passed around and cups of hot chocolate with marshmallows followed.

When the hour of departure drew near, the sophomores were sorry, both because they were having an enjoyable time, and because the snow that a few hours before was brought from the North Pole was no longer snow but—rain.

A. E. F. Club Visits C. I. A.

On Saturday, February the eleventh, at 6:30 P. M., the members of the A. E. F. Club, with their girl friends, went to the C. I. A. As soon as all had arrived at the Cafeteria, the new commander, Mr. Cooper, called them to order, and as names were called, each couple passed into the neatly decorated dining hall.

The invocation was offered by Mr. McDonald. Following this, a delicious luncheon was served, with Mr. Cooper presiding as toastmaster.

Mr. Neely gave a very intrepid prophecy of the club members as he saw them in 1950. Mr. McDonald made a wonderful scientific talk on "The Technique of Possum Hunting," for which his observation and experiments had qualified

him to speak as no other man in the club could, except, perhaps, Squire T. Cook. Then Mr. Murray, in his outbursts of elocution, paid tribute to the ladies. One would never have thought that a man of Mr. Murray's youth could have given such an able psychological discourse on this subject. Next, in a laconic message, C. A. Davis presented "The Problems which Confront the Modern Student of Campustry." Being inexperienced on such a subject and being in the presence of a master, C. J. Neely, he seemed a little uneasy. Then Miss Harrington, who is the only lady member of the A. E. F. Club, made a very much appreciated talk.

In conclusion the happy crowd sang a number of songs and then started on their way back to the Normal.

The Freshman 'Possum Hunt

On Saturday evening, February eighteenth, at 5:30 o'clock, seventy-four tender-hearted freshmen were thrilled when they started into a great forest known as "Anderson's Farm." They were accompanied by Miss Broadfoot and Miss Duggan, who proved to be very pleasing chaperones.

First, they found themselves before a great fire, and for one time in life got all they could eat. The "eats" consisted of hot dogs, buns, pickles, hot coffee, toasted marshmallows, and such like. The leader then told some ghost stories that made everyone shudder with horror.

Soon they heard the dogs barking in the woods not far away and started to them. After walking about ten minutes, the crowd found themselves in the middle of a small graveyard. Several screamed and numbers were heard calling for their mothers.

Many queer things were seen and many queer noises were heard in the cemetery. At first the hunters heard the voice of some one in great distress, and after going back only a short distance they were confronted by spirits. A great white cloud began to rise in front of them. All at once it disappeared in the heavens. The entire crowd was in a spiritual dream, and did not awake until about nine-thirty. They then started for camp again, not noticing that one of the leaders (Miss Broadfoot) was still in the land of the unknown. Cries were made that she had sprained her ankle, and it was found necessary to carry her to a near-by car, when, alas! it was all a joke.

The crowd all left for home, feeling refreshed from the outing and believing that they could stand the final examinations without a shudder.

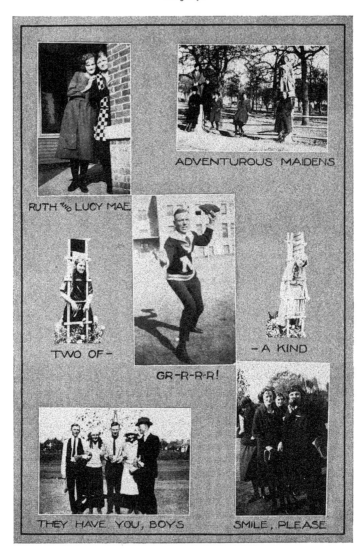

ADVENTUROUS MAIDENS

RUTH and LUCY MAE

TWO OF –

GR-R-R-R!

– A KIND

THEY HAVE YOU, BOYS

SMILE, PLEASE

Dr. John Dewey

Dr. John Dewey of Columbia University, recognized nationally and even internationally as one of the foremost educational leaders of our time, visited the Normal on Saturday, February fourth, under the auspices of the Educational Exchange.

In the afternoon he gave a public lecture to students and townspeople. He spoke of education in China, where he has recently made an extensive investigation. He stressed especially the recent changes in Chinese education, explaining their social and political significance.

In the evening Dr. Dewey was the guest of honor at a banquet, which served as the quarterly meeting of the Educational Exchange. More than one hundred Exchange members and members of the faculty had the opportunity of meeting the great educational master, whose books they had so diligently studied and taught. After the delicious four-course dinner, Mr. Odam, who presided as toastmaster, explained the purpose of the Educational Exchange.

Dr. Dewey made the principal address. He heartily indorsed the work of the Exchange as an educational clearing house which will be instrumental in making teaching an experimental science. The major part of his address consisted of a discussion of the scope of vocational education.

C. L. C. Party

The members of the Current Literature Club gathered at the home of Miss Cora Belle Wilson for one of their socials, and nothing that could make the evening enjoyable for the girls was spared. The decorations were violets and large bouquets of roses and carnations. Miss Mattie Smith played some beautiful selections on the piano, and Victrola numbers were chosen from the records given in the musical contest.

Miss Morley led the girls in playing a number of amusing games. Also, as a pleasant surpsise, she had mastered a trick which she did not forget on this occasion. When in the midst of a game, she suddenly disappeared, but soon returned and called for several of the girls, who followed her into another room. The mystery as to what she did has not been solved yet, but we do know that screams of joyous laughter were heard from that room, and each girl who went

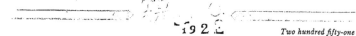

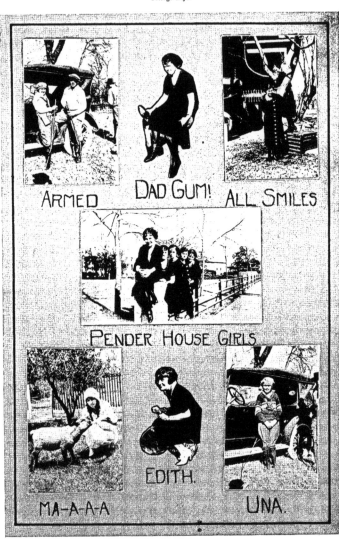

into this mysterious place reports that she knows how to say correctly "Boots without shoes."

About ten o'clock the girls assembled in the beautifully decorated dining room, where Miss Wilson, in her gracious way, served delicious refreshments.

However, the hand of time pointed too soon to the hour of eleven, when all prepared for departure, but not until each had expressed a wish that they might meet more often.

Faculty Club Entertains

On the afternoon of February twentieth, students, dressed in their best, were seen going in different directions to their respective teas, which were given at the homes of Miss Myrtle Brown, Mrs. Pearl C. McCracken, Mr. and Mrs. L. W. Newton, Miss Cora Bell Wilson, Mr. and Mrs. A. S. Keith and Miss Mamie Smith. The teas were given by the Women's Faculty Club, the purpose being for the teachers and students to become acquainted.

The homes were beautifully decorated with cut flowers, ferns and flags. A very gallant little George Washington met the guests at the door, and little Martha smiled her most gracious welcome. The students were ushered to an attractively decorated tea-table, which was presided over by a member of the club dressed in colonial costume.

The guests then entertained themselves for a while by talking with their class-mates and the members of the faculty before bidding George and Martha farewell.

Press Club Members Attend Purple Pig Cabaret

In order to see just what a Bohemian Cabaret looks like and in order to improve their knowledge of the different styles and manners used in such an institution, the Press Club payed a visit to the Purple Pig and found themselves highly entertained. The Pig seemed to have discovered the intention of the famous Club and was very effectively decorated. Large signs such as "Watch the pig," "Don't flirt with the waiters," "Not responsible for parents unaccompanied by their children," and "No minors allowed," together with some wonderful local talent paintings, held prominent places on the wall. The Manager and Head Waiter of the Pig were arrayed in dress suits and gracefully played the part of hosts. The waiters were of Japenese or Chinese origin, judging from their costumes, and were of the flirty female variety. Before the regular course was served, they offered for the entertainment of the visitors a little ditty entitled "I am at home where I hang my hat." This selection met with great approval from the members of the Club, especially from Mr. Woodrow Wilson and Mr. William Bryan.

After the rendition of several musical numbers of the "come and get me" variety, an exciting menu was displayed, exciting because of the fact that wine, beer and whiskey were in prominence. Everyone gave an extensive order and Mr. Masters is reported to have told the waiter that his cellar was about empty. Of the remaining dishes the most prominent was chicken salad, aged in wood; corned beef, while you wait; and fruit salad, spiked with grape juice.

With the feast at an end, the party decided to invade the Open House that happened also to be in session that night, and all, including even the flirty waitresses and the manager, rushed forth and began to parade to the Normal Several were stopped by the officers, Miss Ruby Smith being among these, because of slight disfigurements in their costumes. However the Open House was reached without any serious casualties and the waitresses were duly admired by the house attendants.

At the early hour of twelve the party adjourned and many expressed their desire to return in the morning. However, after the effects of the menu had worn off, the majority were satisfied.

POLITICS

TENSHUN! SALUTE!

ROGER

SHE LIKES IT

ELLIE

Glee Club Turns Things Topsy-Turvy

A casual passerby might have been startled at the appearance of a motley crew of strange creatures with coats and collars buttoned behind and with left shoes on right feet invading the Music Hall one Wednesday evening. Such unusual proceedings were simply the Glee Club's way of having a good time. The guests were greeted at the door by a social committee, who said. "Good-bye, come again." Then they backed upstairs to a cloakroom. When all the guests had assembled, "backwards" refreshments were served and were the occasion of much merriment. Later came games appropriate for the occasion, the chief of which were a backwards grand march and a backwards spelling match.

The backwards refreshments were provoking, of course, but they did not taste half as delicious as the real ones that came later. At the latest permissible hour the guests departed saying, "How do you do! I'm so glad to see you!"

St. Patrick's Day Social

Mrs. Blackburn, a member of the senior class, entertained the seniors on Thursday evening, March sixteenth. As next day was St. Patrick's Day, the committee decided to have a St. Patrick's Day party.

The entertainment committee had everything well planned, and the time passed so quickly that we were all astonished when it was time to go.

There were the hunting of shamrocks, memory contests, spelling matches, and finally the hypnotism of some of the members of the class. Unique prizes were given in all of the contests. The prize that attracted most attention was the bunch of onions won by John Roady.

No better punch was ever made than was served that evening. Every senior will long remember that very pleasant occasion and be grateful to Mrs. Blackburn and the entertainment and refreshment committees for it.

INTERESTED

DREAMING

ROUGH AND READY

WAITING FOR LUNCH

Silver Stripers and Escorts Brave Rain and Mud

The night was bitter cold, but realizing the truth of the old adage about the faint heart and the fair lady, the Silver Stripers packed a sedan with provisions, arranged a convoy of Fords, embarked, and sailed in quest of certain nocturnal marsupials.

IT RAINED ALL DAY THAT NIGHT

Before many knots had been covered, several cases of faint heart developed. However, the ladies were now so far from port that the case was won in spite of this handicap.

After a strenuous voyage the boats came to anchor near the only dry spot in Denton County, a cow shed. Here refreshments were served, and jokes and songs went the rounds. With the aid of smoke from the campfire, all were able to shed tears at the proper time. Also, Miss Dickson favored the group with an appropriate reading, which was greatly appreciated.

At about nine-thirty the convoy lifted anchor and began the homeward voyage in a downpour of rain. The trip proved to be fraught with danger. In fact, one vessel sank her keel in the mud and remained out until an unholy hour of the night. Fortunately for the others, but not for Miss Harrington, the chaperone was on board the distressed vessel.

The College Favorites

Heretofore it has not been the custom of the Editor-in-Chief to announce the results of the college favorite election, but this year we are going to do so.

Not much interest was shown the first few days of the election. It seemed that the students were holding their votes back until they saw who was leading in the contest. In a short time certain candidates began to receive a majority of the votes, and two of the boys and two of the girls were almost certain to be elected. This left two or three candidates rivals for third place, and it can be safely said that it was a hot race. Never in the history of the college favorite elections has the final result for third place of the boys been so close as it was this year. It is indeed unfortunate that there were only three boys to be chosen instead of four.

For the girls, third place was also in doubt until the final votes were counted, but the result was not so close as it was for the boys.

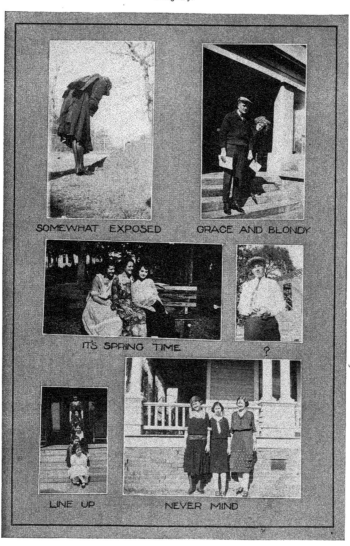

SOMEWHAT EXPOSED   GRACE AND BLONDY

IT'S SPRING TIME   ?

LINE UP   NEVER MIND

The final result of the college favorite contest was as follows:

Girls		Boys	
RUTH CRAWFORD..........	20,280	*First*....HARRY PINKERTON.....	22,880
CLARA COX...............	17,170	*Second*..DAVID A. EDWARDS.....	21,480
HELEN EMBERSON.........	10,970	*Third*...CHARLES LANGFORD....	11,060
WELTA ANGEL............	8,590	*Fourth*...ULYS KNIGHT..........	11,030
RUBYLEA CLEMENT........	7,410	*Fifth*....H. A. PERRYMAN.......	6,690
EFFIE MAE CASH..........	4,050	*Sixth*....C. C. DOAK...........	5,090

Junior Senior Banquet

Saturday evening, March 25, at seven-thirty, the Juniors inaugurated a new college tradition by giving, in the Manual Arts Building, the first annual banquet in honor of the Senior Class.

The guests were ushered into a reception room decorated with the college colors, where they were greeted by Mr. Weeks and Miss Jones, the host and hostess of the evening. Jaunty caps of green crepe paper gave every guest a jovial air.

After an hour of happy conversation the guests marched into the corridor, where the dinner table was laid. Apple blossoms, green streamers, and green candles formed the decorations.

A group of Freshman girls, directed by Miss Pinkney, served a delicious four-course dinner.

Mr. Doak, the toastmaster, likened the student's college career to a relay race. Toasts were drunk to the Manager, Dr. Bruce; the Jockeys, the deans and the teachers; the Blue Ribbon Winners, the Seniors; the Red Ribbon Winners, the Juniors; and the Spectators. Miss Clark and Mr. Anderson spoke in their usual forceful and witty style. Miss Emberson gave two of her delightful readings.

Music was furnished by Cobb's orchestra and by a Junior-Senior Quartette.

After singing the College Song, the guests thanked their hosts for a very happy evening and bade them good night.

T. I. A. A. Championship Cup Displayed in Chapel

The beautiful loving cup that was given by Cullem & Boren to the T. I. A. A. champions arrived at the Normal on March 21 and was displayed in Chapel that morning by Mr. Crutsinger of the Athletic Council. This cup is a trophy for the purpose of keeping in the minds of the generations to come the fact that the first Eagle Team during their first season in the T. I. A. A. carried off the highest honors and won the admiration of the whole state. This team not only won a championship, but, at the same time, made creditable grades in their school work. They came up to the standards which the institutions set, training in both mind and body.

All Gone   All Here

Look Pleasant Please

Juanita   Chums

On the Steps

Don't Fall   Ditto

Luncheon For Eagles

The Normal College basketeers, who took the T. I. A. A. championship, unchallenged, were honor guests at the Kiwanis Club noon luncheon. The six receiving this honor were Pinkerton, McAlister, Knight, West, Perryman, and Edwards.

Mr. St. Clair spoke first and told of the excellent work of the boys and the effort they had put forth to meet with the success they had achieved. He said it is not necessary to put out a winning team at the Normal College, as clean athletics is the first requirement.

Mr. Fouts stressed the importance of physical exercise and said that athletic exercises at the Normal College are primarly to give physical education in its truest sense. He declared that students who engaged in healthful exercises are much easier to discipline. He urged that business men take the time to exercise as they should, declaring that if they do not, they will pay dearly for it sooner or later.

Mr. Crutsinger paid a high tribute to the scholarship and the conduct of the members of the team, reading their grades to show that all passed with a full schedule in addition to making the success they achieved in athletics. He made a plea for the citizenship of the city to aid in keeping down any tendency that the public might have to bet on games, declaring that promiscuous betting would sooner or later destroy athletics.

.Dr. Bruce briefly told of the standard to which athletics must come at the college, declaring that the sport must be absolutely clean, whether a game is ever won, and that the winning of the championship is a secondary consideration.

William Smart, Cowboy, Warrior, Poet, and Funny Man

The students of the Normal were honored with the appearance of Mr. William Smart, an ex-student, in chapel on Saturday, March twenty-fifth. Mr. Smart made a unique picture in his plainsman array, which included boots and everything. Someone made the remark that it was doubtful if any other person with such an unusual dress ever had the privilege of performing on the Normal rostrum.

Bill gave several very interesting readings that had to do with the American Girl and her different moods. He seemed very enthusiastic about girls; in fact they were the dominant feature of his poetry, and doubtless many things were brought to the front that the ordinary observer would not have recognized. One of the local Normal wits made the statement that Mr. Smart should get married, as he was so completely carried away with the fairer sex, but another of the same Normal wits protested because he was of the opinion that Mr. Smart would not be so poetically inspired if he was "running in double harness" with one of his adorable American belles. No, we advise William not to inspect or attempt to study them from close range.

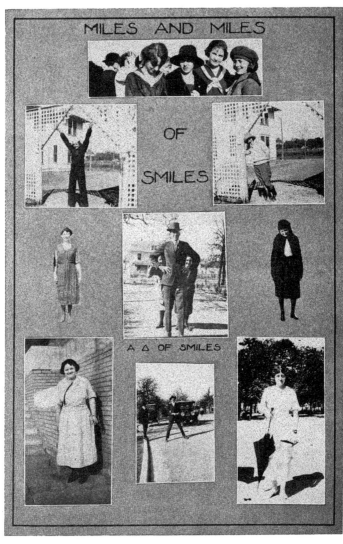

COLLEGE FAVORITES

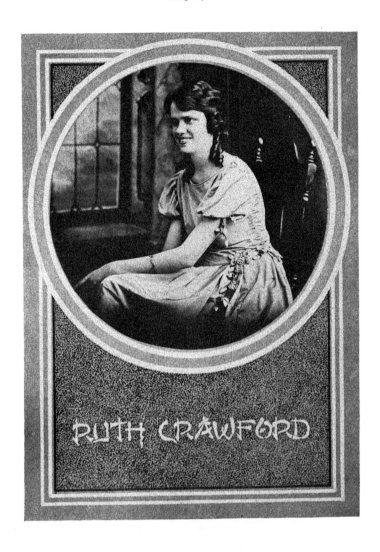

RUTH CRAWFORD

HARRY PINKERTON

CLARA COX

1922

DAVID A. EDWARDS

HELEN EMBERSON

1922

CHARLES LANGFORD

Texas!

Oh endless stretch of grass and sand,
     Texas!
Of artless beauty—sun-scorched land,
     Texas!
Mighty prairies, waving grass,
Home of winter's savage blast.

Yet no heart throbs with gentler beat than thine,
     Texas!
How wondrous wide thy kingdom lies,
     Texas!
Thy freedom born from out the skies,
     Texas!
Distant hills of purple sheen
Painted by the sunset gleam.

To know thee is to know a work of God,
     Texas!
Oh! Endless stretch of grass and sand,
     Texas!
On thee already cities stand,
     Texas!

E'en upon thy patient breast
Works of human hands do rest;
But to the end thy glory will remain,
     Texas!

—Sel.

Remember me and the "Themes"
Just "Sprinkle" Crandall, Texas.

Remember we suffered in Math. 21
at the same time. Effie Springfield—Springtown

[illegible] remember our summer '21 [illegible]
[illegible] history [illegible]
[illegible]
[illegible] Education [illegible]
[illegible]

[illegible] in history [illegible]
[illegible]
[illegible]

[illegible]
[illegible]

My dear Fonnie: [illegible]
[illegible] me Sunday.
[illegible] from you
and [illegible] evening at
[illegible] me [illegible] one evening at
dusk. Where did we go and what did
he think? Remember me as your
friend in every need.
Lee Boyd Midlothian
Tex

Well dear old Fonnie here I am
again. I just never can get thru telling you all the thing I want you to remember. Don't ever forget our day at the
Fleming house. Those nites we listened
to the serenaders and then the
time we were out walking with
Blossom & Chic, and Mr. H came

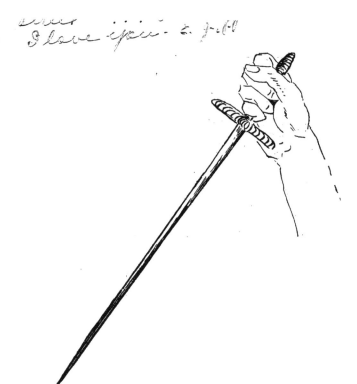

Remember me and the "Themes"
Just "Sprinkle" Crandall, Texas.

Remember we suffered in Math. 21 at the same time. Effie Springfield—Springto[illegible]

[illegible] remember our summer '21 [illegible] [illegible] [illegible] [illegible] [illegible] [illegible] [illegible] [illegible] [illegible] [illegible] [illegible] [illegible] Emancipation [illegible] [illegible] [illegible]

[illegible]

[illegible]

My dear Fonnie:
[illegible] one Sunday [illegible] from you and the short little race [illegible] know who I mean one evening at dusk. where did he go and what did he think? Remember me as your friend in every need.

Lee Boyd Midlothian Tex

Well dear old Fonnie here I am again. I just never can get thru tell-ing you all the thing I want you to re-member. Don't ever forget our day at the Fleming home. Those nites we listen to the serenaders and then the time we were out walking with Blossom & Olin, and Mr. H came

by the cafe. I dodged behind,
out Martha ran off down the
- ??? Always love true - cause
e iou. E.f.f

PERSONALS

F. L. Duggan and R. H. Davis went
to Dallas last Tuesday on business.

Last Sunday Mrs. Lene Compton enjoyed a visit by several of her relatives
from Dallas and Mineola.

Z. B. Cooper was in Gainesville
Monday on business.

E. W. Jackson, a former student and
a senior here, entered school last week.
Mr. Jackson is a well known and popular student. He will take his degree
this summer.

Miss Essie Ball atteneded the dis-
trict meeting of the Women's Clubs
at Denison this week.

Miss Olie Jones has been elected
to the faculty of San Antonio High
School.

J. P. Cooper, a student of the fall
term, is in school again.

Calvin Jones is visiting at the
Normal.

Mrs J. Edwin Taylor will go to
Austin this week with one of her
pupils who is an aspirant for honors
at the state declamation contest.

P. M. Johnston of Valley View
visited here last week end.

Miss Edith Seigler enjoyed a week
end vacation with homefolks.

Miss Harrington has returned from
an extensive trip in the East.

Wendell Oliver is out of the hospital and meting his classes.

Mr. Bennett and Miss Neil of the
board of Regents visited the Normal
last Saturday.

The Vaugham Music Company's
Quartet visited the Normal the first
of this week.

Mable Baskett and Corrine Ewing o
Cleburne spent last week end at hom
Lucy Mae Augustine was in th
hospital last week end, but is no
meeting her classes.

Miss Lillian Van Landingha
visiting friends at the N

ty-three

Dedication

The boys told me all about it,
Told me so I couldn't doubt it,
How upon the fence they sat
　　　Long Ago;
How they sat and smoked and talked
Of the passing damsels, so provoked,
　　　Long Ago.
Now the boys pass by and sigh
As they think of days gone by
　　　Long Ago.

GREETINGS

The foolish ones who did the things
We here retell in black and white,
Finding now the Dagger stings
Declare 'tis falsehood that we write—
For thoughtless speech and careless boast
Have mercy on the Fools we roast!

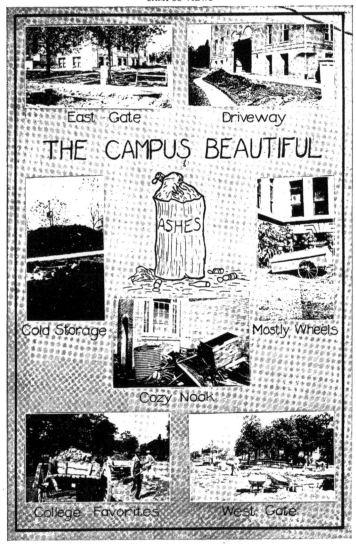

East - Gate   Driveway

THE CAMPUS BEAUTIFUL

ASHES

Cold Storage   Mostly Wheels

Cozy Nook

College Favorites   West Gate

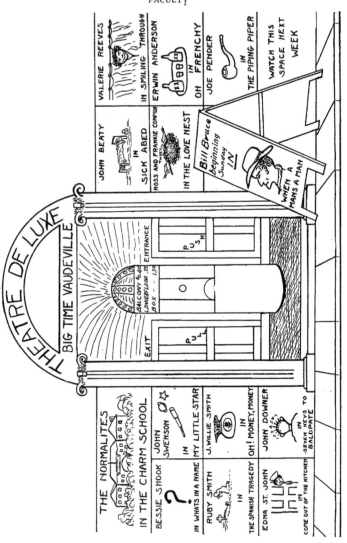

As they used to look

Faculty Feats

Wednesday was a busy day at the North Texas State Normal College. The Butler and the Porter brought in a carload of books. This made the faculty Blair their eyes. Mr. St. Clair said, "Odam, we Haile this Newton of histories; Turner over to the students at once." Miss Harriss with her Broadfoot on the floor exclaimed, "A girl who Masters these will be Looney in a week; they will Downer aspirations." At this Miss Powell Shook Sweet Miss Garrison until her Harris Brown. Then Mr. Floyd made the announcement that the Miller, his aunt, And-er-son had stopped their car on the grass of Dr. Bruce's Normal and were going to Parker there. As this was happening, Mr. Swenson let his Leggett caught in his wheel, for he did not know that Mr. Beaty had Duggan awful hole in the ground, and Mr. Peters had to tell Phil-lips are to Garrison one's words." Mr. McConnell and Mr. Pender volunteered to have the car moved as they had to go anyway to see Wylie about that Blackburn on the campus, but the Smith told them that everything was all right, and order was restored at once.

VARUE ORNDORFF
Her hobby is music,
She plays with such charm,
And dances the while.
Is that any harm?

LOUISE PRESTON
She is a phiz-ed from tip to toes,
And tells it to all whereever she goes.
She plays the game, and plays to win,
But for referees she'll have no men.

L. L. FRITZ
Leroy Fritz put a sign on a cow,
I wonder where that sign is now?
Out in the west near Abilene
Where Simmons College students are
seen.

WILLIS FLOYD
One would have to be a stock or stone
Not to admire his positive tone,
His step, his eyes, his words, his glance
As he reproves others' ignorance.

C. J. NEELY
There was a man in our school,
His name was Charles J. Neely.
On every issue that came up
He turned out Bol-She-Vekie.

GLEN BALCH
There is a Balch boy name Glen,
The way he can lie is a sin.
Sometimes he's gleeful but sometimes
he's sad
Because the women nearly drive him
mad.

HOMER WEEKS
Homer Weeks is so tall and so terribly
thin
I think he has never had a square meal.
But he's a fine guy, and tries hard to
win—
At least he's a winner in the "Old
Virginia Reel."

JIM THOMAS
If all the campus were paper-strewn,
And all the floors were sand;
Old Jim would sweep her up real clean,
For he makes things spick and span.

W. H. BRUCE
His voice was ever soft, gentle, and low,
An excellent thing in a president.

LEIGH PECK
We listen and hear a bird-like call,
Then look and see a bobbed-haired girl;
With poise and charm and queenly
    graces,
She speaks of Ed-Ex in her classes.

HARRY PINKERTON
For short we call him "pink,"
A pretty good name I think.
He goes with a girl named Ruth,
And I know I'm telling the truth
When I say they're a pair
Who can't be beat—so there!

VERNON LEMENS
Good Heavens, his hat,
His new hat, is lost,
Weary hours searching in the rain
Lemens spent all in vain.

R. H. DAVIS
Here Bobbie H. Davis with his smile
    you see;
A man of affairs he aims to be
And leave trivial things to you and me,
While he attains that honored degree.

C. C. DOAK
His love is like a red, red rose,
And also are his cheeks;
But when his lady love appears,
They say he never speaks.

FRITZ HUMPHRIES
Fritz is an awfully good sport,
He always makes good on report;
His card has D's
And plenty of C's
And the girls he does like to court.

BILL COOPER
As you go walking down the street,
A pied-piper you may meet;
His name is Bill, and on this ground
A truer sport will not be found.

Van Camp's (Pork and Beans) Mythical All-American Eleven

The following more notorious than famous men have been selected on the All-American Eleven by Van Camp.

Name.	Position.	Alma Mater
W. C. BLANKENSHIP	*Left End*	Paul Quinn.
JACK GALE	*Left Tackle*	Boston College.
THOMAS B. DAVIS	*Left Guard*	St. John's Chapel.
L. L. FRITZ	*Center*	Mary Allen Seminary.
W. F. BROWN	*Right Guard*	C. I. A.
H. A. ALLGOOD	*Right Tackle*	Terrell Institution.
BEN ROBERTS	*Right End*	Baylor Belton.
THURMAN ADKINS	*Quarter*	St. James' Academy.
JOE HICKMAN	*Right Half*	Prairie View Normal.
CLARENCE JOHNSTON	*Left Half*	Hochaday's Female College.
LEONARD MAXEY	*Full Back*	Gatesville Reformatory.

The men have been chosen for the places for which they seem most unsuited. Van Camp, in choosing this team, has coincided with the judgment of the most important coaches of full-blooded bird dogs. We think it inconsistent to put a personal notice of the respective abilities of each of the above players and therefore shall insert the following:

W. C. Blankenship has the recommendation of being the only football player of 1922 who has fumbled more than 38 times; lost more than 700 yards, and never advanced the ball over 5 inches at one time.

Jack Gale is the only tackle who went through the season without getting in a game. His side line ability was a feature in every game, and many is the time that he was highly cheered by the waterboys.

Thomas B. Davis is the most calm and cool guard that has yet entered the football world. He never loses his head (because it is tied on his shoulders), and rarely ever loses his nerve.

Mr. L. L. Fritz, of the Mary Allen Seminary, undoubtedly is the best center that appeared on the Mary Allen Field this year. Many is the time that the cheers have been so roundly given for him that they completely woke him up.

W. F. Brown, who in previous life was the sideline coach of the swimming team of the College of Housekeeping Industry, is without doubt a good running mate for Davis.

"ATHLETICS"

H. A. Allgood, a former Terrell Institution product who escaped and was not caught, has the reputation of being the only tackle of the season that has withstood the violent plunging of the New York fire horses.

. Ben Roberts, the Baylor Belton heart breaker, has proved very adept on the "Grid," handles himself very gracefully, and does not step on the other peoples' toes. He is without doubt the most self-esteemed of the All-American Eleven.

Thurman Adkins, the unanimous selection for quarter, is a product of the St. James' Academy. He shows admirable headwork and generalship; in fact he was only tackled one time this year, and that was when he was cornered and could not get out of the way. He lost a total of 500 yards.

Joe Hickman, of Prairie View Normal, is the most influential of the football players of 1922. In fact only one good look at his face is enough to turn back the most ambitious runner, and as for carrying the ball himself—well I do not know what he would do, as he never carries it.

Clarence Johnston was perhaps the most popular pupil of Miss Hochaday's Female College before he took up football, and, as in everything else, he made a great success in football. He is tooted as the only man who, during the season, tore only one stocking.

For fullback of this mighty eleven the judges, after careful consideration, have decided upon Mr. Leonard K. Maxey of the Gatesville Reformatory. Mr. Maxey received his former training as gate keeper at basket ball games. This work developed an unusual ability as a pusher, and his vocal cords have reached enormous proportions. Mr. Maxey is probably the most important of this august selection and naturally recalls his importance.

There are several more "Stars" that are probably due a place upon this choice team, but they can not meet the requirements, one of which is that the player chosen must never have had on a football uniform. Some near contestants are Bob Blanks, Levi Martin and Wily Burr.

FORBIDDEN   PASTIME

Saturday Night Open House

"**O**N each Saturday evening from nine until two in the Club Rooms of the Library Building, Dr. Bruce and Miss Clark will be at home to the Faculty and Students of Dr. Bruce's Institution." Thus read the beautifully printed cards issued on our Campus at the beginning of the school year of 1921-22.

The following is one of the typical entertainments as reported to the New York Times:

"Last evening at the hour of nine the Ford limousines began to roll up with combustible sounds in front of the magnificent Library Edifice. Pages, including Tippie Pollon, L. L. Fritz and Heavy Freeman, wearing dainty suits of black cheese cloth, were kept busy assisting gorgeously gowned young ladies, accompanied by their matronly chaperones, into the stately halls. Before entering the Club Rooms the guests retired to the handsome Cloak Room by the way of the electric stairs, which are heavily carpeted with yellow and red matting. Here they were assisted by dainty French maids, including Ilene Compton, Gladys Peeler and Thyra Watson. As they came down the stairs, they were met by their young escorts in vari-colored sweaters, blue, green, and brown trousers, and army shoes. Among the younger guests who carried canes were Messrs. Fred Hughes, Robert Davis, Ralph Patrick, and Carl Young. From the foot of the stairs they, singing the classical selection "The Gang's All Here," trod with prevaricating step into the spacious Club Rooms. The north wing was used for dancing, while the wing on the left was fitted out for the playing of such games as African Golf and Pool. The conservatory was open to those not participating in any of these modes of entertainment. The Hick's Symphony Orchestra, which furnished the music for the evening, was stationed among a background of artistically arranged castor bean stalks intertwined with cactus, in the balcony of the dancing hall. It consisted of 30 pieces. One of the special musical features of the evening was the harmoniously rendered masterpiece, "When You Look in the Heart of a Rose," by Fritz Humphries, harpist, with the obligato played by Jack Gale on the Jazz Whistle. Among those in the orchestra showing rare technique were: John Anderson, saxophone; Bill Myers, French harp; Glen Balch, oboe; S. D. Adams, bugle; Guy Davidson, fiddle; Carol Wilson, kettle drum; Buck Goode, flute, and C. A. Caldwell, steam caliope. The conductor of this orchestra is the famous Dad Pender, for many years the student of Sousa and Ypoye. In the many alluring nooks and alcoves of this room marked off by graceful festoons of sunflowers, delicious hot buttermilk with mint wafers, was served throughout the evening. A delightful interpretation of "Spring" was given by Leigh Peck and Bill Cooper. The special dance of the evening awarded the most favor was "The Russian Ballet" by Clifton Doak. He was presented with a handsome shaving mug.

"COLLEGE LIFE"

In the other rooms tables were set for two hundred players. Each table was decorated with a kerosene lamp the smoke from which added a charm to the atmosphere of the evening. Dr. S. B. Neff won high score at Pool and was awarded a bottle of Swenson's Hair Tonic.

Many beautiful gowned lasses were seen during the evening. Among these may be mentioned Miss Irene Duncan, wearing an artistic tan middy suit, with an alluring picture hat of white felt and a corsage of old maids. Miss Louise Stout wore a brown jersey gown. Her hair was most becomingly arranged in the latest mode, dog-ears; her evening wrap was an elaborate green sweater. Miss Texanna Wilkerson was gowned in a blue serge skirt and a white sweater, embroidered in a red "T," with three red stripes interwoven in the sleeve. Her evening hat was a tam-o-shanter of red and white broadcloth. The hostess, Miss Clark, wore a dainty navy blue tricotine coat suit with a white lace mantilla. She carried an arm bouquet of bachelor buttons and delightfully handled a palm leaf fan.

When two o'clock came the young debutantes with their sedate chaperones departed to their separate Sorority Houses. Dr. Bruce extended a gracious invitation to the young men to remain until daybreak to enjoy with him cubebs, beer, and cheese, and games of pool and billiards.

Among the eminent guests of the evening were: Mr. Homer Weeks favoring Miss Valeria Reeves; Mr. Tracy Hays with Miss Myrtle Brown; Mr. C. P. Jones with Miss Emma Phillips; Mr. C. J. Nealy with Miss Coralie Garrison; Mr. Willis Floyd with Miss Clara Morely; Mr. Bob Blanks with Miss Mary Sweet, and Mr. Harry Pinkerton with Miss Myrtle Williams. Chaperones that were prominent during the social affair were: Hazel Kirkpatrick, Alice Riggs, Mary Jones, Karin Rowan, Lillian Elder, and Martha Roan.

I Love You

You ask me why I love you,
You want to know just why;
My heart beats fast when you are near,
And oftentimes I sigh.

You wonder when I hold you
And look into your eyes
There are no words at my command
I dream of paradise.

No other reason can I give
I love you just because I do,
You are the whole wide world to me
I live to love Just You.

—*Exchange.*

No ⁓ Never

Do I ever catch that air
With my girlie oh so fair?
No ⁓ Never.

Do I get to hold her hand
Does she even know I can?
No ⁓ Never.

Do I ever get to love
Underneath the moon above?
No ⁓ Never.

Do I give that good night kiss
To the sweetest little miss?
No ⁓ Never.

Do I have any time to think
When I see the ten-thirty wink?
No ⁓ Never.

Do you think that I'll make good?
Is there any one that could?
No ⁓ Never.

T.C.

STARS
OF THE
SUMMER
SKIES

The Greatest Disaster in the History of the Normal

New Victims Daily

The student body is so strongly in love with the "indoor sport" of chapel going, and the force of habit had fixed itself so firmly during the first three months of school, that when the students returned from that two weeks of holiday hilarity and found the old chapel marked with a large sign saying "Danger! Closed for repairs," they congregated at the base of the stairs in protest, and then a gallant young enthusiast in the person of Guy Davidson started a drive. The students followed, rushing past the placard with the same reckless disregard of danger that had characterized the Xmas drinking of horrible "home brew" and the midnight ride in the tin Lizzie on New Year's night.

Soon the "Fish," the "Preps," and the "Whatnots" began to file in in the same old way. There was the same "rattling of paper," "tramping of toes" and "rhythmic clapping of dainty hands," as of old, but all of a sudden the Doctor himself, at the risk of his life, mounted the platform, which by this time had begun to sway upon its slender props. What he said in his excitement will not do to print now that we are all cool and sober again. But he pleaded in vain for them to disband; Bob Blanks, a staunch believer in daily chapel exercises, introduced a resolution to hold chapel at all hazards. The resolution was adopted. The Doctor withdrew, and chapel proceeded according to "Hagle," save without the usual annoy of faculty supervisers.

"COLLEGE LIFE"

It developed later that a falling brick had wrecked the bell which tells of the passing of time. Of course no one noticed the lateness of the hour until the dinner bells began to ring, and of course a second rush was precipitated.

When the authorities learned that the hall had been vacated, they called on the A. E. F. to put up a barricade of wire entanglements about the doors. And since then none but the bravest have been able to gain access to the "Sanctum Sanctorum." However, each morning it is necessary to disentangle some victims who have given up their lives in an heroic attempt to make the tri-weekly pilgrimage.

Geometry

Prop: If you love your girl, your girl loves you.
Given: You love your girl.
To Prove: She loves you.

Proof

1. All the world loves a lover.—Shakespeare.
2. Your girl is all the world to you.—Self-Evident.
3. Hence your girl equals the world.—Things equal to the same thing are equal to one another.
4. Hence your girls loves a lover.
5. You are a lover.
Therefore, Your girl loves you.
"   , If you love your girl, your girl loves you.—Q. E. D.

Freshman: I see in this book that fish are a good brain food.
Senior: Then you had better eat a whale.

Ethel Bunch: Gladys, we can work Sunday and Sunday night.
John Anderson: Why I thought I would get a date with one of you Sunday night.
Gladys Peeler: I sometimes change my mind.
John Anderson: Can't you take a joke.

Miss Garison (late at the game): What is the score?
Mr. Porter: Nothing and nothing.
Miss Garison: Thank goodness I didn't miss anything.

Campus Chat

| Much Volume | On Time | Limited Circulation |

MIRACLE OF THE AGE OC-CURS IN THE DENTON NORMAL

The students of Dr. Bruce's College all rushed wildly to the Normal Cafe. This was the scene, on last Wednesday evening, of the greatest wonder this age has ever known. The commotion was so great that the proprietors were compelled to close the doors of the Cafe to prevent a stampede. Many students fainted and all of the doctors in Denton were kept busy restoring the swooning people. Ever since this marvelous occurrence has taken place, the entire school has been in a turmoil and all classes have been dismissed.

The great miracle has transpired!—BOB BLANKS had a NICKEL.

CHAPEL PROGRAM

1. Tues. Student drill in entering and leaving auditorium. B. E. Looney.

2. Thurs. Boys Y. M. C. A. aesthetic dancing demonstration.

3. Sat. Assembly Singing—ragtime. Song leader—Miss Reeves.

On account of serious injuries about the head, received in the season's first basket ball game (against Southwestern), the captain of the team, Mr. Harry Pinkerton, will be unable to play any more this season. The entire school extends its sympathy to him, and trusts that his recovery will be soon and complete.

MODERN ARCHITECTURE OR THE EIGHTH WONDER OF THE WORLD

It has long been the belief among great builders that the "Ne Plus Ultra" of their art had been reached. Of course such achievements as the Brooklyn Bridge, the Woolworth Building, and the Panama Canal are strictly modern, but in their construction there was used no principle of architecture or engineering that had not been used for ages. Modern man has only been able to put together the old ideas in greater mass than ever before.

As is true with most revolutionizing discoveries, the sensation of this age came not from a renowned inventor, but from an unexpected source. It happened that while a ruin at the Normal was being repaired under the direction of our president, a new principle was applied.

In spite of all effort at secrecy the discovery was noised abroad, and before the work was completed, the Normal was having many visitors, among them Dr. Butcher, president of the Normal at Emporia, Kan. At sight of the work he exclaimed, "This gives me new light. I shall return to Kansas, 'brace up,' and employ this principle."

The latest information from Europe is that the new principle is being used extensively on that continent; many of the ruins of the late war have already been "braced up." The leaning Tower of Pisa also is to be saved from collapse. However, it is feared that few American tourists will be interested in that tower in the future, for the original "eighth wonder of the world" is to be seen at Denton, in our own country.

It is rumored that the State Legislature is to erect a new Administration Building here, and thus preserve the present one that future generations may see what a great Texan has contributed to the world.

RESOLUTIONS

Whereas, we have labored inevitably and in great turmoil, under the guidance of the faculty. Therefore be it

Resolved and hoped that in this age of wireless telegraphy, horseless carriages, fireless cookers, kickless beer, and danceless proms, that some benefactor of mankind will establish a Faculty-less School. If this can be done, many athletes may play ball and students attain certificates.

Be it further resolved, that a copy of these resolutions be presented to the Men's Haculty Club and the Women's Caculty Club.

Signed:

Guy Davidson
Bob Planks
Harry Pinkerton
Pat Neff Roberts
W. H. Simms.

Why does Ollie Jones have such pink cheeks and such fluffy hair this spring?

Curious one

CAMPUS CHAT

Results of Conscientious Efforts.

THE STAFF

Chief Petty Officer— John Anderson.

Pharmacist—Fred Hughes.

Ensign—Fritz Humphreys.

Lieut., Jr. Grade—W. L. Murray.

Lieut.—Glen O Balch.

Lieut., Com. — Elizabeth Adams.

Com.—C. C. Doak.

Cap.—Charles Langford.

Rear Admiral—Ethel Bunch.

EDITORIAL

THE COLIDGE INSTRUKTER

If you want to know a peculiar sort of persunige, try an meet up with sum Colidge Instrukter. They are both mail and femail, and they look a rite smart like other people, but looks is decivin. Instruckters are sum times called purfesers, being mails most gineraly speaking. Its diferunt with the mails and femails for to looky at the mails you wouldn't no wheather he was weded or not. A few aint yet. With the femails you can purt near guess rite wen you've seen them onst. If you lisened to them in class you would take them to be religus heirs and a few are. We aint got much rite to kritisise them tho, bekose allmost no Colidge cood run far without none of them.

Usely they has purty manners and its seldom that they get ruff with the gurls and boys. Nobody has much greater nolidge than a Instruckter. I have herd sum purfessers talk about favarit arthurs which most of them has. Sum Colidge instructors have got cinse and its wonder they are proud of it.

Students should exkuse their falts kose probibile before they was instruckters they was skolers themselfs onst.

POINT SYSTEM CREDITS GIVEN TO OFFICERS OF N. T. S. N. STUDENTS

Honors of office and consequent labors should be distributed among students.

The point system is designed so that any student may aggregate 20 points a term.

A. MAJOR OFFICES:

The major offices are those offices to which students are elected or appointed for the year.

Group 1. Those majoring in campustry, or loafing, President of the K. O. E.'s and Score board keeper: 15 points per term.

Group 2. Yell leader: 12 points.

Group 3. Sec't. Bulletin Board: 11 points.

Group 4. President of Concrete Packers Association and President of Lounge Lizards Organization: 10 points.

B. MINOR OFFICERS

Group 1. President of Star Navy Chewing Club: 8 points.

Group 2. President I-Hate-Me-Club: 5 points.

Group 3. President Students' Barber Shop: 4 points.

Group 4. Janitor of Mail Boxes: Letter - Inspectors: 1 point.

NATURE'S OWN REMEDY

Doctor Cronkrite's latest scientific achievement: Hair restorer. Guaranteed to grow hair on door knobs. Any style or color.

Carried by all Hardware dealers.

Manufactured by

Dr. C. L. Cardwell,
hair tonic chemist.

WEEK OF TROUBLES

The year had gloomily begun,
For poor Senior, a poor man's Sun.

He was beset with bills and duns
And he had very little Mon.

"This cash," said he, "won't pay my dues;
I've nothing but ones and Tues."

A bright thought struck him and he said,
"A rich man's daughter I will Wed."

But when he paid his court to her,
She lisped, but firmly said, "No Thur."

"Alas," he said, "then I must die."
His soul went where they say souls, Fri.

They found his gloves, his coat and hat,
And the coroner upon them Sat.

LOWER CLASSMEN ATTACK SENIOR

SUMMONED FOR HAZING

The ears of Mr. Fred Hughes were bitten and severely injured by Misses Aubra Jones and Dickie Dickson on last Saturday afternoon in the Yucca office. The case was reported by the following witnesses: Carl Young, Gladys Peeler and Ethel Bunch. Mr. Hughes was taken at once to the College Infirmary in "Wylie's" Ambulance. He is reported in a very serious condition, but Doctor Bruce, who was called immediately to diagnose the injuries, said that his recovery would be complete, except for a small part of his right ear, which has entirely disappeared. This was the ear attacked by Aubra Jones. The two offendants will be tried for Hazing before Judge Butler and his court.

Miss Clark called a meeting, today at Chapel period, of the officers of the Mary Arden Club to consult with Messrs. Blackburn and Vitz, noted architects from New York City, in regard to the erection of the Mary Arden Lodge. They will lay the foundations of this Lodge sometime within the next five years.

WANTED—Rules of etiquette. I have just started out in society.

Harry Pinkerton.

WANTED—For next Saturday night's Open House, a 42 partner who won't spend all of her time looking at other boys.

Loyd Vickers.

SOCIETY

Following the elaborate wedding ceremony at 4:30 on the morning of Saturday, Feb. 31, which made one of Miss Leigh Peck and Mr. John Hansard, a number of the intimate friends of the bride and groom went to the Union Station to wish them a happy wedding tour in the solitude of the Arctic Region. Mr. and Mrs. Hansard were conveyed to the station in the handsome limousine of Mr. Fred Hughes. The remainder of the wedding party rode in the Galloping Goose, driven by Dr. William Bruce's chauffeur, Mr. Little Boy Venable. The bride wore an attractive traveling suit of green jersey with accessories to harmonize. The young couple were showered with rice, old shoes, and confetti, as they ascended to the train. As the train slowly pulled out, the charming bride, with a last kiss for all it signified, threw her beautiful bouquet of wild roses to her friends. It was caught by her beloved friend, Miss Lillian Elder, the rumor of whose engagement to Mr. Vernon Lemens has begun to circulate.

Mr. and Mrs. Hansard will remain in the Arctics until the opening of the 1922 fall session of the N. T. S. N. C. when they both expect to take places on the college faculty. Their many friends extend to them a wish for a joyful sail on the good ship matrimony.

Those included in the party were: Mr. and Mrs. Ted Riggs Sizemore, Mr. and Mrs. I. B. Martin Griffith, Mr. and Mrs. Loren Leverett McCray, Misses Sou Clay, Edith Martin, Enie Bess Carlton, Clara Cox and Lillian Elder; Messrs. Punch Fulton, W. C. Blankenship, Wm. Boyd, C. L. Caldwell and Guy Davidson.

WANTED—Adequate means of telling the difference between the Lees and the Regans.

Jno. Hansard.

N. T. S. N. C.

To the Student: If after reading carefully the following rules, you are unwilling to comply with them, do not enroll.

1. Absence: If a student should desire at any time to leave the city, please do not trouble the dean by asking for a "Leave of absence," but just catch the first train out of town.

2. Study Nights: Sunday, Wednesday, and Saturday nights are study nights. On these nights students must be in their rooms preparing their lessons between supper and curfew.

3. Cuts: Students must not report to any one class more than three times each term. The remainder of the classes are considered as cuts.

4. Chapel Attendance: Students must not enter the auditorium without written permission. If permission has been granted, the front sections must not be occupied, and no student shall sit in the same seat twice.

5. Entertainment and Company: (a) If a young lady student wishes to receive attentions from the young men students of the Normal, she must obtain from Joe Nealy, head of the Department of Campustry, a written permission.

(b) All picnics and swimming parties must be held on Sunday, and no teacher is allowed to be present at any of those affairs.

6. Joy Riding: Cars may be rented at all hours of the day and night from Dr. Bruce, Mr. Pender or Miss Morley, for the purpose of joy-riding. Each student must arrange a time within each 24 hours for a joy-ride, preferably between the hours of seven-thirty p. m. and five-thirty a. m.

7. Curfew: Every student is expected to be away from his boarding place within fifteen minutes after curfew has rung.

TEST YOUR MEMORY

Come to the Music Memory contest.

Friday night in Auditorium. Boys Glee Club will shine in the latest song hit—"In sellin' kindlin' wood to get along."

NOTICE TO SERENADERS

Don't sing beneath Viva Rabins' window—she has a bucket of water waiting for you.

WEST AND DAVIDSON

Detectives at law.

We hunt 'em down and try 'em ourselves.

TIPPIE POLLAN

Announces his candidacy for heavyweight favorite for the college.

NEXT LYCEUM NUMBER

Major Bumozken—Arctic explorer will lecture on the Polar Regions.   Surprising-Something new.

READ THE LATEST SNAPPY STORY

"I'm Through with the Women Forever," by Glen O. Balch.

ACTIVITY TICKETS FOR SALE

Gets your early—avoid the rush. Leonard Maxey.

FOR SALE TO THE HIGHEST BIDDER

Four barrels of Rollicking Spirits, six bottles of High Life, one yard of unbroken rules.   All practically new.   I'm retiring from business to enjoy private life with my sister. Jonsey Jones.

ATTENTION ATHLETES

Just on market. Yeast guaranteed to raise all failing grades to the required average. Experts have proved its power since the fall of 1921,

LESSONS IN CLEANING STAIRWAYS WITH GLUE BRUSHES

Pansy Varnell
Ethel Bunch
Emily Hayes.
Demonstration Cottage.

THE WORM WILL TURN

The above picture shows the sign which was swiped by a representative of Simmons College when their football team was here.   A Simmons College student was kind enough to take the above picture and send it to us. Thanks, old top. But what we were going to say was this: While they won a football game from us by the measley score of 7-0 and swiped the sign from us, we fixed 'em in basket ball. The score of the first game was 29-13 in favor of the Normal, and the second game 48-17 ditto. Yes, boy, our team eliminated them from the T. I. A. A. championship race.   Ah, sweet revenge was ours—The worm will turn.

PERSONALS

Lee Preston visited Grace Frazell at the Carson House last week-end.

Dickie Dickson confessed to the Editor that she has been proposed to three times.   Oh, she is such a child

This year John Hansard has settled down until he acts as if he would make a good "slave" for some woman.   What's the matter, John?

I say, Angel, didja ever snuggle up close tu knight when you were sitting in the porch swing and stroke his curly hair, and tell him what a wonderful Basket Ball star he was? I say, didja?

MISS CLARK GIVES INTERESTING TALK ON "THINGS NO GIRL CAN AFFORD TO DO"

Briefly summarized the following points were made in Miss Clark's excellent mass meeting talk.

1.   To miss any gossip.

2.   To be so quiet that no one turns to look at her.

3.   To lose her chewing gum in some rush.

4.   To sit in the light with young men.

5.   To wear out her hat by putting it on to go down town.

6.   To make herself conspicuous by not using paint and powder.

7.   To regard in any way the rights of other people.

Harry Pinkerton plays forty-two with Louise Preston every Saturday night at the open house.

Mr. Ben Roberts went out to see I. A. and she wasn't at home.

Miss Mamie Smith sang in chapel last Tuesday morning..

Mr. W. H. Sims is making his annual visit to the Normal to make the Yucca campaign for the Lees.

They say the Mary Ardens and C. L. C.'s don't get along very well.   I wonder what a girl does when she belongs to both 'em?

Judge Venable says he has kept company with 35 girls and has been proposed to twice since he has been in school here. Yeah, Weeks, and Fritz too.   We have a chance yet if he told the truth.

Wonder why the A. E. F. Club doesn't have a party or banquet or something?   They haven't had one this week.

It is reported that Joe Neely cussed out loud one time and somebody heard him.   We wonder.

I. B. Griffith was seen talking to Helen Martin a few days ago. We are glad they have made up.

Who is that blonde who runs around with J. A. McDonald?

FORD GIVEN AWAY

To the person guessing the correct age of Mr. Clarence Brown.   Watch his actions, listen to his conversation, and observe the top of his head; then make your guess.
Open House Committee.

Found in John Anderson's Waste Basket

My dearest John,

The great love I bore for you increases daily. The more I see of you the more you appear in my eyes an object of contempt. I feel myself in every way disposed and determined to hate you. I could assure you that I never intend to love you. Our last conversation has left an impression on my mind, which by no means impressed me of a high standard of your character. Your temper would make me entirely too unhappy, and if you and I were united I would expect nothing but hatred of my friends added to the everlasting displeasure of living with you. I have indeed a heart to bestow, but I do not desire you to imagine it at your service I could not give to anyone more inconsistant and capricious than myself and be capable of doing justice to myself and family. I think that you know that I speak sincerely, and if you will do me the favor of avoiding me you need not trouble yourself about answering this letter as you are always full of wit, humor, and good sense.

I am so adverse to you that it is impossible for me to be

Your affectionate Sweetheart,
Mary

Read only underscored words.

The Distinguished (Looking) New Student

A Ford coupe pulled up at Dyche's corner.

"Stranger, would you like to see our campus?" These words came from within. In a jiffy there were two handsome young men where there had been but one before, and the flivver moved west.

"Friend, of course you do not know it, but that corner is the rottenest hole in Denton. Those buzzards on the fence are congregated for no other purpose than to defile their mouths and ruin their eyes—(pause)--by smoking those nasty cigarettes. The sheriff and two deputies are unable to keep that corner clear. The building on the right is neither a dance hall or a cabaret; if it were, the corner which we have just left would be deserted. The jazz music that you hear is made by Martin and Hills' electric piano. A student has just succeeded in rolling a slug down the slot, proving that an education gained here is highly practical.

The manual training department teaches how to make the slugs.

"Those are not fire escapes that you see leading from that building. They are more in the order of architectural crutches. Dr.

Bruce is seeking patent protection on the idea. The principal involved is already being seized the world over.

"You mean the big house? That is the home of a most wonderful woman. She is the only person in these parts

who can manage the big squeeze. In recognition of her success the students have named an important club in her honor.

"The gate we are about to enter was designed by Hugo John Peter, and erected by student (volunteer) labor. It is considered (by some) to be a work of art. The tiny boy leaning

"WORSE AND WORSE."

against the post is not a motion picture comedian, but only a well-known college athlete.

"The group under the trees is a class in campustry. The atmosphere here is ideal for the pursuance of this most important study. On our left you see a congregation of important men. The tall blond is an admiral. He is renowned as a college politician.

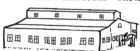

"That horrible odor doesn't indicate that this is a suburb of north Ft. Worth; neither does the smoke from the windows indicate that the science building is on fire. Mr. Masters is only demonstrating diffusion with sulphated hydrogen. The feet hanging from the upper window show that a Freshman has mistaken the odor, and after an unsuccessful attempt to kill the scent by rubbing with a dead rabbit has hung them out to air.

"Keep your seat, I assure you there is no danger. Those wails are not of a damsel in distress, but only a victim of the reading department taking vocal gymnastics. Oh no, they are not crazy—they all do that way.

"We will now turn to our right, circle the campus and visit the gymnasium. On the corner you see Harmony Hall, where they teach certain select students the art of vocal torture, which they practice on the rest of us.

"Now look to the right —the building with the tall chimney is used in heating the air which circulates to the other buildings. With the exception of the boys' literary societies, it holds the record for generating more hot air per minute than any other organization about the school.

"On our left you see the only genuine human experiment station in the United States. The first wooden building on the same side is where the girls practice domestic "science," while the building on the corner is designed and equipped to take care of the physical man in any lapse of life's journey from the cradle to the grave. The building on the right co-operates in this great work. Here they do all amateur work in wood, stone and metal. The cradles, the boxes, and the concrete monuments are furnished here.

"We now turn south. The frame building you see on the hill is the barracks, or gymnasium. The tall man stooping to enter plays forward on the basket ball team. The San Marcos folks said he was seven feet five inches tall.

"Now friend, I belong to the XY society. I would be glad if you would become a member of this society."

Just then our guest let it be known that he was not a student at all, but just a common "jelly-bean."

The Ford made record speed back to the corner, where it dumped half of its cargo.

> Young Homer got down on his knees
> And besought a young love for a squeeze.
> She gave him a note—
> And on it she wrote,
> "I never do flirt with the hes."

"CRACKS AT THE CROWD."

Famous Sayings by Famous People

Every speaker in chapel—"It gives me great pleasure to look into your bright and happy faces."

John Roady—"Buy a Yucca."

Joe Neely—"Unprintable."

Gladys Peeler—"Hello, Captain."

Mr. Crutsinger—"Brother Hood, are you ready to testify today?"

Mr. Vitz—"What I want is results."

Mrs. McCracken—"No talking in the Library."

Leonard Maxey—"Where's your ticket?"

Helen Emberson—"Wash my face; wash my face."

Judge Venable—"When I was at State University" or "When I was in France."

Ben Roberts—"Say, you fellers didn't have any good debaters out at the Normal last year, did you? I am coming out and defeat San Marcos this year."

Guy Davidson—"Hello, Freshman."

Mr. Looney—"The rear sections pass first."

Charles Langford—"Fifteen for Eagles; One, Two, Three."

Doc. Bruce—"Now pay close attention to what I am going to say."

Dad Pender—"Do you catch it?"

Ted Sizemore—"What I want to know is, who in the --- told I swiped that pennant."

Mr. Downer—"Reserve your seats for the Lyceum early. We have a rare treat in store for you."

Acknowledgment

NOW THAT the last page of the Yucca is complete and we have a minute to pause and look back over what we have accomplished in the way of editing and managing a college annual, it occurs to us that there is something left undone.

It would be utterly impossible to publish a college annual the size of the Yucca in a year's time without the co-operation of scores of people. We have had this co-operation, and it has been the largest factor in aiding the staff to place this volume of the Yucca in your hand.

We have had most satisfactory service from the Southwestern Engraving Company of Fort Worth and the Hugh Stephens Printing Company of Jefferson City, Missouri. Our interests have been their interests at all times, and we have been treated most courteously by the representatives of these companies.

We wish to take this means of thanking the students who patiently solicited subscriptions for the annual. Especially do we recognize the valuable services of the Captains of the Hornets and Wasps, Aubra Jones and Ted Sizemore, and of John Roady and Pansy Varnell, who sold 75 annuals each.

Of course the Editor is grateful to the whole staff for the great amount of time each has spent in gathering and preparing the material for this edition, but he wishes especially to thank Leon Taliaferro, who toiled many hours to carry out the editor's idea in designing and decorating the class panels, the kodak pages, and the college favorite panels.

We wish to thank the Faculty supervisor of the Yucca, Miss Mary Sweet, for the free "censorship" she has given us this year. The staff is of the opinion that we have more nearly made this a student publication than has any staff of previous years.

We take pleasure in recommending our advertisers to you. Many of these firms have suffered financial reverses this year, but they believe in the Yucca and have contributed toward making it a financial success. Let us patronize our advertisers and convince them that it pays to advertise in the Yucca.

To every one who contributed toward making the 1922 Yucca a success, from the president of the college to the janitor who sweeps out the publication's office—WE THANK YOU!

We wish you "Bon Voyage" on the sea of life.

Sincerely yours,

CARL R. YOUNG,
Editor-in-Chief.

JOHN S. ANDERSON,
Business Manager.

PEACEFUL(?) SLUMBER.

"I'll remember you"

My Favorite Faculty Members

Jessie Ruby - Grammar "You [illegible] [illegible] much [illegible] [illegible] [illegible] [illegible] you as a Teacher. Ha! Ha!!"

J. E. [illegible], Math. [illegible] Madame, [illegible]

Beulah Ann Harris Fairbury Neb. Gym."

Olive Hallett [illegible] [illegible]. [illegible] of fun.

[illegible]

Lillian Watkins - [illegible] [illegible] a pleasure

My Girl Friends

Don't forget — Mildred Caudhill,
Whitewright, Texas

Ellen Thacker. [illegible] ... [illegible]
[illegible]
[illegible]
[illegible]
[illegible]
[illegible]
[illegible]
[illegible]

Mary Love, Cairness, Texas.
Fannie, old sport, what are
you going to do this sum-
mer in Evermon? Now for
my ~~sake~~ sleep and sleep
and then sleep some more.
Remember me as one who
will remember you always.
Birt Halloway. Avery, Texas.
I know it is not very much
consolation after we reach the age
of 20. But when u are blue.
"Remember all things comes to those ~~who~~" wait.
Beulah [illegible], [illegible]
Annie [illegible]

Dear Barbut, I come home
about 6o-clock,
When you go back to Ever.
ness, running and don't
under had our supper
first.

Mary Cooper, 516 ave. Denton, Texas.
Don't forget the bobbed haired girl that
worked by your side in cooking, for
I never shall forget you. I love you too.
Lillie Gillespie, Sunny, Texas.
"Fannie, I'll always remember you by y
pleasant smile and charming ways."
Pauline Barton, Denton, Texas.
Emma Jane Pryor. Longview.
Dearest Fannie. Always remember me as one who love
you. Also remember the days
we have spent together. Fannie
we held out through thick and
thin. I love you lots.
I shall always remember "my little
friend" across the street. Lilliar Maisenzill
"little friend who made this", think of me and
send me a letter when you want to. too
B. Ivey Meador, Denton, Tex, 513 Bernard

My Girl Friends

Laura Wilhelm, Vernon, Texas.
"Always remember the walk
we took the other day and
your shoe hurt your little foot."
Barbara Tom - Hallsville, Tex.
Always remember me in
connection with Mr. McKay
and History 22.
Mary Sloan Lamesa Texas
A good old friend in Math. 20.
"My Dear chief Jim.
So sorry, but I have
none out of my long group."
Hazel Hurd
Hallsville, Tex.
Opal Shipley Grandale Texas
"We know how to cook, don't we!"
Zylla Maye Misenhimer, Lillian &
Please don't forget our friend —
Willie Mae Hammack. Liberty, Tex.
Remember the campfire. Mr. Misen-
himer, L. 24.
Gladys Fleming, Misenhimer, Lillian, say
"When you are in Hereafter. How
you will to talk about us. Ft. Worth
Texas."

My Boy Friends

Tracy Hayes, Gustine Txas.
"Ah, great day I can't use my
head."

K C O Ellington, Frizzler, Texas.
Said the coyote to owl, Hurry, Howdy do
Said the owl to the coyote, What, What in
hell do that to you.

B Cronkrite. — Lillian Zepa
L S Fritz Mc Kinney, I feel sure
that I missed much in not knowing
who you were earlier, best wishes, keep thinking
[illegible]
"I hope you make "A" in mathics"

R F Hodge, Chatfield Texas
Do you know where any good
looking girls are.

Mays Caterence, Jermyn Tex.
[illegible]
[illegible]
[illegible]

F B Parnell Sulphur Springs Tex.
Jack Bailey Shelbyville Tex.

My Boy Friends

Albert E. Bell, Dillian Jean.
"Classmates in English 22"

C.S. Wilkinson, Dentos, Texas,
"A friend of the old maid"

Raymond Patterson, Tampa
"Remember me" Pat
9th. Blankenship, Ovala, Texas
"I am glad to know. Remember you."

My ~~Boy~~ Friends

Mullin Texas

Well Dick's leaving

you make Math. 22

Sarah Wren — Boyd Texas

"Tomorrow exam

on Math 22 tomorrow. You

have my sympathy"

Bertha Lee Casstevens, Lillian, Tex.

Fonnie, ole dear, do you remember

the good times we had last summer?

you tell 'em we went to the

Cascade and "tried on" slippers too.

Well Fonnie, anyway don't

forget me and that I do not

live very far from you, so

come to see me sometime.

Billie Burtis Frankston Tex

"Fonnie, can we sew and can

we cook? I'll say we can. Don't

forget me."

Annie Myra Spencer Thomas, Texas

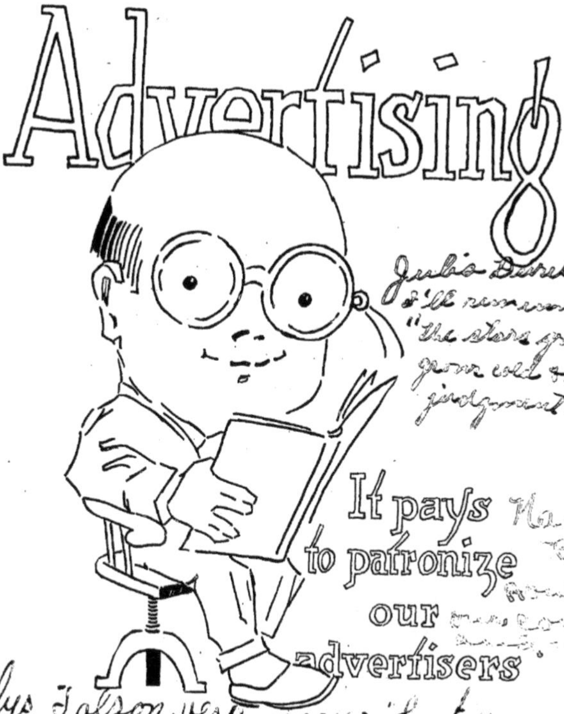

Gladys Folson, Vera Texas

WATKINS' STUDIO

We thank you for the many favors this year and here are our best wishes for you wherever you go.

The pictures in this Annual were made by us and you can get extra prints, at any time, by writing us. We will be only too glad to take care of your order by mail.

We would also like to do your kodak finishing and can take care of it in a prompt way—cash on delivery by mail.

N. A. WATKINS & WIFE

Denton, Texas.

—*at* Hertzberg's

the Diamond House of Texas since 1878

Correct Gifts for Every Occasion

—DIAMONDS
—WATCHES
—JEWELRY
—FRATERNITY
 EMBLEMS
—CLASS PINS
 and RINGS

THE reputation of the · House of Hertzberg has stood the test of time ******* for close on half a century there has been no higher assurance of absolute satisfaction and highest quality than the Hertzberg name

HERTZBERG
JEWELRY CO.

"At the

Sign of

the Clock"

HOUSTON ST., CORNER ST. MARY'S ST.
SAN ANTONIO, TEXAS

Three hundred fifteen

A STUDY IN BACKS. NAME IT?

WHO? BY THE GATE—

WOODS HOUSE GANG SMILE

RUSSELL-GRAY-JONES CO.

EVERYTHING

IN STUDENT'S DISTINCTIVE APPAREL

"Service With a Smile"

RUSSELL-GRAY-JONES CO.
The Home of HART SCHAFFNER & MARX

PRINCESS THEATRE

*W*E claim the Picture Theatre which selects its entertainments carefully and is an influence for better citizenship. All our time and energy are used to get the best and cleanest pictures to be had.

We Thank You.

J. M. VIVION
Owner and Manager

"25 Years of Service"

To the Faculty and Multitudes of Students of the North Texas State Normal College:

During this period of a quarter of a century it has been our constant endeavor to offer our large patronage merchandise of known value and style moderately priced.

We will appreciate your mail orders for any item, large or small—it may be shoes, a certain dress pattern, millinery or ready-to-wear. In either case your wants will have our immediate attention.

W. B. McClurkan & Company
"Denton's Largest Department Store"

FIRST NATIONAL BANK
DENTON   TEXAS

CAPITAL and SURPLUS
$100,000.00

FIRST NATIONAL BANK
Wants Your Business

Three hundred eighteen

When You Need Anything Dry Cleaned or Dyed, Phone 31

For many years now—ever since we have been in business—we have been dubbed the official Normal College Students' Dry Cleaner and Dyer.

THERE'S A REASON, TOO

Prompt, efficient service, coupled with unfailing courtesy and the highest grade of work, has made our establishment popular with both students and faculty. We admit that we cater to your trade and will do everything in our power to merit a continuance of same.

We make a specialty of one-day service without extra charge. We pay return parcel post charges on out of town work. Try us.

EAST SIDE TAILOR SHOP

You cannot estimate the value of courteous treatment until someone with less appreciation than we treats you otherwise

COURTESY IS ONE OF THE ASSETS OF THIS BANK

May We Have Your Account

FIRST GUARANTY STATE BANK

OFFICERS AND DIRECTORS

M. L. MARTIN, *President*
W. C. ORR, *Vice-President*
W. E. SMOOT, *Cashier*
JNO. W. CRAIN, *Asst. Cashier*
R. W. BASS, *Asst. Cashier*

W. D. BUTTLER
P. E. McDONALD
O. M. CURTIS
CHAS. H. SMOOT
J. W. STUART
J. M. EVANS

Kraft Built
College Annuals

THE largest, uniquely equipped modern plant in the west, specializing in the designing and production of "Kraft Built College Annuals." ❧Our Service Department renders expert assistance and supplies the staffs with a complete system of blank forms, together with a handsome ninety-page Manual Guide dealing with the latest methods in advertising campaigns, business and editorial system for College Annual production. ❧Helpful advice and ideas are given on art work for Opening Pages, Division Sheets, Borders, View Sections, and other Annual sections, combining Kraft Built bindings, inks, and papers into beautiful and artistic books—SUCCESSFULLY EDITED AND FINANCED. ❧Write for estimates and samples to The Hugh Stephens Company, College Printing Department, Jefferson City, Missouri.

"Such Unexpected Flavor Combinations"

is the verdict of everyone who eats

TEXAS GIRL CHOCOLATES

"Sweetest in 48 States"

15 Complete Assortments   101 Distinct Varieties

Rich, Flowing Centers of Real Fruits and Nuts, Dipped in
Highest Grade of Chocolate Coating

Aristocracy and Creme de la Creme

Assortments contain the choicest goodies of

TEXAS GIRL CHOCOLATES

A most complete line of 5c and 10c packages   Our guarantee with every box

BROWN'S
DALLAS

Three hundred twenty-five

Second Year Team—Class Champions, 1922

Top row—PALSER, NASH, BROADFOOT (*Coach*), TAYLOR, BORDERS
Front row—HANCOCK, McGLOTHLIN (*Captain*), WILSON

WE take this means of thanking you for your patronage while you were attending the NORTH TEXAS NORMAL COLLEGE, and want you to know if we could at any time send you shoes or hose, of which you will always find we have the latest in styles; it would be more than a pleasure for us to do so.

DOSSEY & HOLLOWAY

Just to Remind You of

CALL ON US WHEN IN FORT WORTH

Write for anything wanted when you can't come

We Serve Through the Mail

SERVICE   QUALITY

We Strive to Please

NORMAL PHARMACY

O. R. DYCHE

HARRIS-KOENIG
HARDWARE CO.

N. E. CORNER SQUARE

PHONE 119   DENTON, TEXAS

Three hundred twenty-eight

PRINTING A STUDY

Three hundred thirty

The Friends of EDUCATION

The Dallas Morning News
The Dallas (Evening) Journal
The Dallas Semi-Weekly Farm News
The Galveston Daily News
The Galveston Semi-Weekly Farm News

POPULAR TEXT BOOKS

By North Texas State Normal College Authors

Elements of plane and solid geometry
By W. H. BRUCE

Victory Historical Map and Outline Books
By L. W. NEWTON

Problems in Elementary Woodworking
By HUGO J. P. VITZ

*Write us for detail information concerning
these and other modern text books*

THE SOUTHERN PUBLISHING CO.   DALLAS, TEXAS

Southern School-Book Depository

311-15 PRESTON STREET

DALLAS   TEXAS

From A Friend

Three hundred thirty-three